The Writing Life

The Writing Life

The Hopwood Lectures, Fifth Series

Edited and with an Introduction by
Nicholas Delbanco

ANN ARBOR

THE UNIVERSITY OF MICHIGAN PRESS

Published in the United States of America by
The University of Michigan Press
Manufactured in the United States of America
♾ Printed on acid-free paper

2003 2002 2001 2000 4 3 2 1

A version of the introduction, "Scribble, Scribble, Scribble," first appeared in *Harper's Magazine* (January 1999). All other essays first appeared in *Michigan Quarterly Review.*

A CIP catalog record for this book is available from the British Library.

Library of Congress Cataloging-in-Publication Data applied for
ISBN 0-472-09717-2 (cloth : alk. paper)
ISBN 0-472-06717-6 (pbk. : alk. paper)

Contents

Introduction: Scribble, Scribble, Scribble

Nicholas Delbanco

In 1990, as Chair of the Hopwood Awards Committee, I edited a volume of Selected Hopwood Lectures, *Speaking of Writing*. That omnibus text includes essays delivered viva voce from 1932 to 1989—from Robert Morss Lovett, the first Hopwood speaker, to Francine du Plessix Gray. Since then, and at the annual award ceremony here in Ann Arbor in April, we have heard from William Kennedy, Robert Hass, Richard Ford, Roger Rosenblatt, Geoffrey Wolff, Diane Johnson, Louise Glück, Philip Levine and John Barth. Their talks are here reprinted and they make an impressive roster of artists who stand at the lectern in Rackham Auditorium at semester's end. As I wrote in the previous volume, "To claim a common denominator for these essays is to risk reductiveness; they deal with no single shared theme. Yet the speakers share an assumption that literature matters, and vitally, to the culture it reports on and sustains."

The audience is young, engaged, and those who enter the Hopwood contest are serious, win or lose. It is my happy task to hand out money—nearly one-and-a-half million dollars has been dispersed to student practitioners by the Hopwood Committee—then introduce the writer and sit down. Year after year the advice is provocative; year after year I've been proud to play MC. And it's of course unseemly to introduce a speaker at greater length than will be the speech, so mostly what I try to do is keep my introduction brief. The lectures will speak for themselves. They were intended to. But in the pages that follow I run on unabashedly; I can't invite myself, of course, to deliver a formal Hopwood address but want to join a conversation that has been such a pleasure to witness and such an instruction to hear.

Here, therefore, are my own first questions for a text that ends with John Barth's "Further Questions" as the new century starts. Ideally the monologues that follow do constitute a dialogue—a kind of contrapuntal discourse on *The Writing Life*.

"Another damned, thick, square book! Always scribble, scribble, scribble! Eh, Mr. Gibbon?" So remarked the Duke of Gloucester, in a put-down and a send-up both at once. For in this story, surely, the speaker gets the best of it, turning from his slight acquaintance bent above the desk to matters that *do* matter: the purchase of horseflesh, the vote on Home Rule, the decanter of Château D'Yquem. His is the sort of epigrammatic utterance to which there can be no rejoinder, the clean hit and quick-killing witticism: once-over-lightly and leave.

But let us linger awhile. Let's first assume that the phrase is correct—that it wasn't improved in the telling, or written long after the fact. It isn't clear, however, if this formed a part of sustained conversation or an effective one-liner—if it came at the end or the start of a meeting. Was there an answer made? What might the answer have been? The jibe is formulated as a question, after all; perhaps it's a matter of mere intonation and the rising inflection gave way to a snort. Or proffered pinch of snuff. Or inch of first-rate port.

It wouldn't work as well, of course, were Gibbon not still famous. "Scribble, scribble, eh, Mr. Smith?" has neither the ring of authority nor the power to amuse. What counts is the disparity between that mighty finished thing, *The Decline and Fall of the Roman Empire,* and the diminished process: children and illiterates may scribble, but not our renowned historian. He was too *serious,* surely; his ornamental sentences and massive buttressed paragraphs required an adept of penmanship: calligraphy, perhaps. And at the least a quill pen.

So the disjunction *should* amuse. It was intended to. "Still writing, Mr. Gibbon?" is a polite question merely, and would not make us laugh. As Noel Coward, with his own "talent to amuse," observed: "If you've any mind at all, Gibbon's divine *Decline and Fall* sounds pretty flimsy, no more than a whimsy. By way of contrast, on Thursday last, I went to a marvellous party. . . ."

All this by way of preface to a set of questions I think it fair to ask: why bother with the enterprise of poetry or prose? Can writing be taught and by everyone learned? How does one evaluate texts? Will a first-rate teacher produce a first-rate student and which are the terms of improvement; what's good, what's better, best?

Even such questions may well seem elitist, and the Duke of Gloucester has come to rule the day. For who in truth believes that language can be taught? We learned it long ago, not consciously, and by now it's closer to breathing and walking than a skill we need to have honed. The rules that still pertain to study of a foreign language no longer apply to our own native tongue; words like "ablative" or "accusative" have been thrown out of school. Yet English is the present lingua franca and very few now recognize what those words signify or how their meaning in translation has been changed. French was the language of diplomacy for centuries; not now. I don't mean by this to engage in some high-flown lament as to the lowering of standards, but only to observe that "rhetoric" is in and of itself a suspect word. Where once it meant the art of expressive speech or discourse it now seems an indulgence to avoid. Nor is a rhetorical question one that entails a reply.

In this age of electronics—with easy access to the personal computer and cell phone and home media center, television, voice mail and e-mail and the rest—it's simple enough to get by without books. Not to mention the subsidiary skills of literacy: a knowledge of grammar and ease with articulate speech. Few adults today recite poems by heart; no one past adolescence still composes verse but those who make of it a lifelong and poorly paid vocation. Too, the art of letter writing is almost wholly defunct. The powerful have language produced for them by an oxymoronic *speechwriter;* the teleprompter is the sine qua non of our nightly news. Few new houses have bookshelves built in, and even the assiduous consumer will but scratch the surface of a season's available work.

Let's say—a generous estimate—that we read a book a week and continue to do so for forty years. This would amount to two thousand books, not a thirtieth part of the titles offered by the industry each year. Not to mention those which are reprinted and outlast a single publishing season and the shredder's blade. Or take the extreme and scholarly case. Say we read five books a week for fifty years and keep them in our head and on the shelf. This would surely suggest a literate person, one of the chosen few. Yet the number's still a small one: twelve thousand five hundred volumes, not the first floor of a library in any self-respecting town. And most of us don't read that much or read that long, and after twenty years or so we might as well begin again for all we can remember of our childhood texts.

Some writers take pleasure in secondhand bookstores, those dusty upstairs rooms and barns where their predecessors molder and, perhaps, a long-sought or a half-remembered volume may be found. Some busily hunt their own work on such shelves or delight in new discovery and add to a collection. I do not. I'm haunted by the spectre of these abandoned pages and those who wrote them when quick, not yet dead: a graveyard of language gone mute. It is, I think, proof negative of the folly of ambition; even Gibbon—still a household name?—is largely now remembered as the butt of another man's joke.

Nonetheless we may with justification surmise—this footnoted in Dr. Johnson, Volume II, by the solicitous and quasi-ubiquitous Boswell, in whose honor we here momentarily deploy an imitative Gibbonesque and soi-disant Johnsonian diction if not rhetoric, the *ur*-text beyond us as well as behind—that the response in due and proper course would have arrived in the affirmative, and that our author glanced up from his work desk, polishing his spectacles, inclining his head, smiling, weary, purse-lipped, pretending affability, secure in the foreknowledge of attainment and the satisfaction of the day's work done, and well, and perhaps already knowing that this Duke so fatuously baiting him would fade into obscurity, or not so much obscurity as that particular limbo reserved for the querulous (the self-proclaimed wit and the buttonholing and lapel-pulling windy bore, the meddlesome person from Porlock), a semi-circle and half-hell of indeterminate and quasi-anonymous not to say parenthetical identification (which Duke of Gloucester was it, after all, and how old or young and in what private home or club and when did they discuss Home Rule?) whereas he himself, the historian *soi-même,* the great aggrieved and weary Edward Gibbon, would outlast this upright and chattering sedulous ape, survive this jape, from boot to cape caparisoned in language, lovely language, always scribble, scribble, scribble, yes indeed.

Well, that's one way to put it. Here's another. Edward Gibbon wrote a lot, and one day an acquaintance asked him why. What's the point, pal, after all? You write too much, says the Duke. Outside it's cold, it's sleeting maybe, rattling at the windows of the club, (the Reform, the Garrick, the Athenaeum?) and the poor are huddled to the coal grate by the porter's door in the alley where the night soil reeks and horseshit steams. In that corner barely visible beyond the mullioned window behold a toothless rag-wreathed creature squabbling with the dogs for scraps while in the library we light our pipes, and later on there's dancing girls, my favorite is Mimi, why bother with that quill pen, Ed, when she's so much more entertaining to tickle with this ostrich feather instead? Do pass the bottle, there's a good fellow, and sample a bit of this Stilton, I had it sent down particularly, now what were we saying? Oh yes. Let me give you a piece of advice. All work and no play keeps the devil away, and there's deviltry in Mimi and, what's the expression, you're a great one for expressions, the devil's in the details and the details are what's fun.

Some years ago I had a conversation that I carry with me, still, as a cautionary tale. I stopped a farmer—call him Everett Saunders—on his tractor in the road. The lane was little traveled, dirt and dusty; it was July. He had been commended to me as a man who would cut wood, mow fields, do neighborly labor for a fair price. I had more land than I could handle and was in any case incompetent at farming; I needed help. Everett recognized me also. In that village any stranger was discussed.

"You're the one they call Nick," he said, and killed the motor and lit up his pipe. Puffing, he kept silent while I blundered on about which cows I'd pasture in which field, what kind of grass I planned to plant and how much he could cut. When I said I was a college teacher and therefore—transparent excuse!—couldn't farm full time, he perked up. He had seven children; one of them was soon to enter nursing school. We had a long discussion, and he took eager part in it: the benefits of education, the value of a degree, the methodology of teaching, the particular instruction that his daughter would receive, the scholarship money available, the high cost of tuition, the risk and yield and loss. He was behind her, Everett said, behind her all the way.

Emboldened by such newfound friendship, I offered a personal truth. "I'm a college teacher," I announced, "but that's not all I do. What I really love is writing, I'm a writer, I write books."

His eyes glazed. "Books," he said. He knocked his pipe bowl empty on the steering wheel. "Don't mean nothing to me." He started the tractor and left. For the five years that I worked at my three novels of the farmer's life—the Sherbrookes trilogy—I tried to remember his answer, that lack of interest and cap-tipping scorn. "Don't mean nothing," say our characters, "to me."

Or because he is not used to playing second fiddle in any such ensemble—because *his* is the title here and *he* has commissioned the performance—Gloucester clears his throat. Loudly. To embark upon that most tedious of exercises, self-justification. Wherein he will avail himself of the very weapon of his seated adversary and also wield the pen. He will call for ink and paper and produce a monograph on ancestor worship in Mesopotamia, on weaving in the Hebrides, primogeniture in Spain. He will demonstrate once and for all that the gulf that spreads between them—the man of words and man of action—is, to the sufficiently capacious intellect, a dimple of a ditch. He will write his own essay, compose his own speech.

It is not difficult.

It takes no time at all.

It is the sort of challenge a gentleman cannot refuse: the casual yet causal deployment of skills, the anagrammatic mustering of just the word or, as those froggies call it, *le mot juste.*

He clears his throat.

The stars, could he see them, are bright.

The gutter has been sluiced.

Then, no doubt thinking better of the prospect, disheartened in advance by what he can already taste is and as the ash of half-felicitous and wholly pointless utterance, the rhetorical trope and ripe rodomontade whose tripping comeliness upon the tongue leaves triflers but the taste of tripe, that busy tinkering with language for which he does not give a tinker's damn, he lifts his white kid gloves instead from the proffered silver salver.

And shrugs himself into his greatcoat and nods at the footman, preparing to leave.

For he is promised elsewhere, and time and tide won't wait.

There's a matter of some urgency and—though he be too discreet to confide it—state.

Still, to have the last word is too great a temptation and Gloucester can't resist.

Who can refuse an exit line; what actor willingly gives his back to the curtain when the curtain falls?

One final rejoinder, perhaps.

One small last thing to say.

Therefore surrounded by his retinue and negligently, condescendingly addressing himself again to Gibbon, the Duke avers: I hunt, I ride, I court and fence and dance with more accomplishment than you. I have many achievements of which you don't dream and to which you cannot attain. When walking in the gallery or counting in the countinghouse I stand or sit at ease; the highborn and the low approach and turn by turn require money, counsel, comfort in the battlefield or the bed at night. To each his own, sir: you to your inkwell and I to my volume of cares.

All authors have been students; many teach. We have an industry of advice on everything from investment portfolios to spiritual growth to weight loss to golf swings and how to correct what's gone wrong. Bookstores bulk large with "how-to" books, and books on writing are now no exception; instruction rules the day. Where there used to be just Strunk and White, or Fowler's *Modern English Usage,* there are programs to purchase, from spell-check to syntax, that guarantee an improved vocabulary in thirty nanoseconds, much less thirty days.

The academy, of late, has served as patron for the writer much the way the court or wealthy individual did before. It is, I would guess—though I know of no statistical survey—the largest employer of those who make their life if not their living by the pen. But the poet in the Renaissance, or even in the early years of this present century (consider Yeats and Rilke and how often they traveled from country house to castle), did not imagine that their verse would prove literally ennobling; it was a business, this "singing school," and not one that granted degrees. We have moved some distance from the notion of a guild, but all those MFA programs and writing festivals and writers' conferences that spring up in such profusion subscribe at least implicitly to the idea of advancement; apprentice yourself to an author and earn your working papers until you too attract apprentices who come in turn to class.

And though the current wave of interest in writing programs is likely to crest and diminish, it will no doubt accumulate once more. The desire of the human animal to express itself in language is inhering and enduring; from the first mark incised in stone to the contemporary microchip we want to fashion utterance and leave it behind us for others to scan. "In the beginning was the word" may be a loose translation, but it does serve as genesis for the people of the book, and ibis-headed Thoth is god both of speech and its scribes.

The only way to learn one's art—a craftsman's paradox—is through backbreaking labor that must not seem like work. Like the dubber in a foreign-language film who most succeeds when no one knows he's around. Or like those Zen masters of the martial arts. After the body has been trained to achievement, trained so that what earlier seemed impossible is difficult, difficult habitual, and the habitual easy—at the point where everything is instinct, true mastery begins. The highest *dan* cannot be attained; the highest attainable *dan* is reached through meditation. So we have the spectacle of the ancient jiu-jitsu *sensei,* crumbled into the carapace of age, sitting on his tatami mat in the sun. And a disciple—full of health and radiant muscularity—comes up and assumes an attack stance and says, "Master, I must kill you now," and raises the axe. But the *sensei* pulls out the rug from under his student's feet.

Therefore I urge myself to practice, trusting to the notion of perfection later on. We are all of us apprenticed to a fast-vanishing guild; the species is endangered and much mastery is specious nowadays. Hunt that old codger in the sun, I tell myself, but don't swing your axe if you find him. Look up his sleeves with reverence, and keep at a respectful distance from the mat.

Which books are *square;* when did the word come to signify *dull;* will the O.E.D. here help?

Why is the book not damned, thick and rectangular; does this suggest a conscious or unconscious inattention on the speaker's part?

Does he, I mean, not know the distinction or not bother with the difference between rectangular and square?

Between the trapezoid and tetrahedron and the parallelopiped and the cube?

That large text and this small.

There are many more scenarios and half-fleshed possibilities; the Duke has made Mrs. Gibbon his mistress; the Duke's daughter displays a marked fondness for Gibbon but the match would be unthinkable; the two of them were once Apostles in their shared salad days.

They have met often; they've only now been introduced; this is the start of a new friendship or rupture of an old.

It would be easy enough to construct a play with these two as dramatis personae and to provide a prior or a subsequent encounter.

But our patience wears thin and the rest wears away: it is only this line that remains.

For whatever the context, whatever the tone (teasing, combative, querulous?) the phrase survives. "Another damned, thick, square book!"

It's what we have that endures.

My elder brother is a doctor, and a very good one. We may have our disagreements as to politics or wine, but he is always right in matters medical and I follow his advice. Some time ago I had the habit of puns, and the more atrocious the better; no subject escaped my sonorous attention or grasping verbal reach.

An example: if the review of a novel by a *prose pro* were negative, we would have a *conte contretemps.* The contraction of professional to "pro" is more or less self-evident, as is the contraction of convict to "con." But how prosaic it would be to limit oneself to mere English, even if it be the mother tongue, or bitter mother, *mère amère;* why shouldn't the contrary also prove true? To be pro or con, as in the voice-vote yea or nay, is not the same as to be a paid baseball player or criminal who perpetrates a trick. The translation of *les cons* is unprintable in these proper pages, but contract it to *leçons* and it seems merely instructive. English profits from the sidelong glances of such pigeon-kicking pidgin-quickening; the echoic aspect of language, its echolalic resonance, proved important to the bard of Beowulf as well as, later, Joyce. Rejoice. It would be easy equally to play on "gibbon" as a primate's name and perhaps ancestral ape or cousin of the cadet branch, as in gorilla, orangutan, mandril, chimpanzee, a monkey who batters at Shakespeare on his battered Smith-Corona beneath the gibbous moon.

Then my brother said that punning was a clinical condition, and I asked of what.

Of tertiary syphilis, he told me, and the paresis induced by the final stage of the disease. If a patient comes into your office, he said, who's punning uncontrollably, you know that the patient's in trouble, and bad. I sputtered, I spluttered; he grinned. I have made few atrocious puns since.

It's fun, nevertheless, such babble; we ought admit to that. If there weren't pure pleasure in the way words edge up against each other, in the way paragraphs fit, in learning how katechresis can prove serviceable—then we'd all have to be a higher and bloodier minded bunch. Because the average wage is maybe a penny a page, or dime each twenty hours; the average reward is anonymity. If your name is well enough known to be taken, then it's likely to be so in vain, or *mispelled;* vanity and sottishness and the deep paralysis of repetition await those who truly succeed. We dream of influence; it's effluence instead. Those who hunt success too consciously are conscious of too little else; those to whom it comes unbidden do its bidding soon. It's easy to inveigh against the scribbler's rotten lot, to say we're blessed or cursed or necessary prophets without honor and too few who're honorably with. But there are other professions, and most professional wordsmiths could find some other job. They don't; they won't; why not? One answer is, it's fun.

Or perhaps there's an admission here, a wry-faced yet modest avowal: the Duke doesn't care to read. He never got the hang of it, he never acquired the taste. He has, as someone once remarked though in another context, small Latin and less Greek. And therefore this grave history that Gibbon labored hard to write is something of a threat to Gloucester, or at least an implicit reproach: you understand what I fail to, sir, what accrues to your credit lies lodged to my debt. You command language as I do the servants, you make a phrase sing whilst I cough. A proper man—so goes the old saying—can build a house, can plant a field and father sons and write a book. The three first tasks present no difficulty to me, sir. But *language,* there's the rub.

From the Duke of Gloucester we may move to the Comte de Montesquieu, whose definition of the writing life equally endures:

> Author: A fool who, not content with having bored those who have lived with him, insists on tormenting the generations to come.

In 1985 I published a book on the Beaux Arts Trio. A nonfiction study of chamber musicians, it presented a problem of voice. I added and invented nothing but translated much. The three artists (Isidore Cohen, violin; Bernard Greenhouse, cello, and Menahem Pressler, piano) were more expressive in music than speech. Not for them the terminology of music criticism or any discussion of theory; they would demonstrate a phrase by singing or playing rather than articulating it. Greenhouse is by nature reticent and Pressler, although voluble, not native to English. The injunction "speak in tongues" became a comic babble when I transcribed tapes. I spent a week with them at La Chaux-de-Fonds—a small town in Switzerland where they made albums for Philips Records. In conjunction with the Italian violist, Bruno Giuranna, the members of the trio recorded the two Mozart piano quartets. The engineers were Dutch, the piano tuner German. As Giuranna observed, "When musicians must discuss a piece, it's a very bad sign. You must have it in your head, of course, but play it with your heart."

Here is a verbatim rendering of discourse, from my notes and tapes. They were in rehearsal; I will not try to indicate who was speaking when. "*Nun,* take it from D. Wubba wubba wubba wubba. *Ich habe quasi improvisatore ici*. You follow my bowing and I follow yours. Wubba wubba. You lose the whole effect of that *piano* after playing *forte* for fourteen bars through. Last night I tried going up, today I go down—the take-over shouldn't sound as if now it's *me*—but lead up, please. I'd like a little less activity on that boobooooobooboo. Would it be too Beethoveny if you played it bumbumbum; is there a wedge on each note? No, it's the bush that burns underneath.

"It's *nicht gut*. It's march music. Where do you put this accent on the phrase? Where do you want it? On the downbeat. Then be careful of the A-flat. The first five notes after the slurred note, could you start a little lighter? That sounds *vermisscht*. Did you hit the low E-flat? I'm playing it; fantastic, at the end, how he takes away the chord and leaves the E-flat clear for the piano. Let's try it once just as written, *nun,* from D."

Rounded off, there were fifty hours of such talk for the one completed hour of performance. The recording is, I believe, eloquent, the language clearly not. Or, more precisely, my role was to evoke the nature of the enterprise in a language faithful to but sufficiently distant from the original to be more than mere transcription. This was a particular problem of reportage and, perhaps, extreme. But it seems to me an emblem of the novelist's ongoing task: we witness and translate.

What we choose to witness is, of course, of consequence; the sounds of a three-fingered amateur ukelele player would be less rewarding to study than those of the Beaux Arts Trio. The death of Anna Karenina has more enduring resonance than does the death of a flea. Yet Tolstoy's transcendent novel took flight from a newspaper story; James built elaborate fictions upon the chance dinner-party remark. It is seldom possible to gauge beforehand what will prove a fruitful topic or which anecdote will fire the imagination; some matters move us, some do not. The writer gleans wind scraps; he listens whenever he can. Each day is full of instances; what counts, as with all stimuli, is the sympathetic response.

This is not to say the writer need do research of the spirit or backbreaking kind. It should not be forced. Here Gibbon cannot help us much, for his entire enterprise depends upon the research done and information accrued. Will the discerning reader note that, very well, I contradict myself, that Gibbon and Gloucester now fuse at the lip? The poet and the novelist deploy a methodology separate from the historian's and this is appropriate; we don't play tennis with a basketball or football with a bat. Nonfiction and the mass-market saga rely on data principally; factchecking is but one component of the imagination's work. There are better road maps to Dublin than the novel *Ulysses,* and we would believe the snowstorm in "The Dead" if it had not snowed that day.

But if a character's a carpenter his author has to know the difference between a jig and bandsaw; if the heroine's an Avon lady we should know what products she sells. When we use up our store of available data—the stuff of childhood, then youth—the professional writer is left with one profession to describe. Then it grows imperative (or every book would be about its own construction) for us to practice "reach."

My argument therefore resolves into this: when the self-conscious witness casts about for subject matter, he should pay attention to the visible, audible world. Inflection is as various as fingerprints. We should train our ears and accents as do actors if we hope to play more than one part. The intonation of "self-conscious," for example, has grown pejorative but few would feel the same of the Greek injunction, "Know thyself." Self-consciousness is necessary; it is not sufficient. "Another blessed thin rectangular book!" The voice of the accomplished author will be a chorale.

And finally, there are two modifiers we must finally address. Both sentences begin with an exasperated, aspirated *A. Another* and *Always* bespeak true compulsion, and not so much upon the speaker's as the writer's part. What *is* it, we should ask ourselves, that keeps him keeping on? Too many trees have been levelled to furnish this ream of blank paper and realm of fool's gold; too much language has been already expended on the Roman Empire. It is enough, my *semblable*—oh, surely, much more than enough. That those who do not know their history are doomed but to repeat it but compounds the problem: this repetition compulsion of sitting to the work of words day after day after day. *"Another damned, thick, square book! Always scribble, scribble, scribble! Eh, Mr. Gibbon?"* How is it he replies?

I write because I must.

I write for the reasons adduced here above: the fun of it, the comfort, the sense of commonality, the chance to shape what's shapeless and know what is not known.

I write because what's said is fleeting although we imagine it lasts.

And because the word "adduced" itself stands rooted in the fading past; it means "brought forward, led towards," and we will not advance as species without the advantage of hindsight, foresight: both retrospect and prospect fused in what's composed.

For the shape of it, the sound of it though silent, the feel of the print on the page.

Out of habit too, and hard to break, the taste and smell of it, the way steam rises from my coffee cup before dawn when I wake to dream, the sixth if only intermittently available sense that just beyond the reach of these first five is a republic of letters where the lords of language walk.

I write because *Another* means we've been this way before.

I write in the hope that *Always* means we'll go this way again.

And that you will read.

Writers and Their Songs

William Kennedy

I was working as a newspaperman when I was drafted into the army during the Korean war, and I decided to write a continuing column about it called This New Army, which was what everybody was calling that same old army in those days. I wrote about how unbelievably stupid sergeants and corporals were, how unspeakably dreadful army food was, and how very peculiarly the general behaved when he noticed I was marching out of step.

When these columns were published back in Glens Falls, New York, enlistments in this new army dropped to zero, the first time I changed the world with my writing. This change was testified to by the local doomsday recruiting sergeant, who packaged off my clippings, along with a formal complaint, to Fort Benning, Georgia, where I was taking basic training in a heavy-weapons company of the Fourth Infantry Division. Because I could type, somebody had made me the company clerk, and so I also got to answer the phone. A call came in one day and guess who it was for? Me. The major who ran the Division's public information office was calling.

"Kennedy," he said to me, "that was a funny column you wrote the other day about the general."

"Thank you, Major," I said. "I'm glad you liked it."

"I didn't say I liked it and don't write any more." And then he added, after a pause, "Come up and see me and maybe I'll give you a job."

Well I did, and he did, and for the next two years I spent my days writing for army newspapers in the U.S. and Germany—Germany because our Fourth Division became the first American troop unit to go back to Europe after World War II. I was also thrown in with the literate and subliterate malcontents who populated the public information section, most of them also draftees and ex-newsmen, and four, including

---

The Hopwood Lecture, 1990

me, aspirants to writing of a different order—short stories, novels, films, plays; we weren't particular.

These years were seminal for me, the period in which I dove head first into literature. One of my great pals was a brilliant newsman from Mississippi who had not only seen and talked to Satchmo, he had actually attended a lecture by William Faulkner. Closer than that to the Empyrean no man I knew had ever ventured. Four or five nights a week we would gather in our enlisted men's club in Frankfurt, arguing, over heilbock and doppelbock, the relative merits of Sherwood Anderson, Hemingway, Dos Passos, Steinbeck, Caldwell, Fitzgerald, Mailer, Algren, Katherine Anne Porter, Flannery O'Connor, James Jones, Irwin Shaw, Thomas Wolfe. "Wolfe said it all but Faulkner said it better," was the youthful anthem from Mississippi.

I tried then and since to read everything that all these writers ever wrote and I have succeeded, perhaps by half, though I'm still working on Faulkner. I also began writing what I thought of as serious short fiction. I had written stories in college, all derivative and blithering, but now I was beginning to match myself against these maestros I'd been reading. At first I was such an amateur I couldn't even imitate them, but in the year or two after I left the army I managed to write dialogue that sounded very like Hemingway and John O'Hara, I could describe the contents of a kitchen refrigerator just like Thomas Wolfe, I could use intelligent obscenity just like Mailer, I could keep a sentence running around the block, just like Faulkner. But where was Kennedy?

I came to loathe the stories, as did my family, my friends, and fiction editors from coast to coast. Nevertheless, by diving into literature I had baptized myself as a writer. I have since come to look upon this as a religious experience; not because of its holiness, for as a profession it is more profane than sacred, but because of its enmeshment with the Catholic Church's supernatural virtues of faith, hope, and charity—as I had learned them.

Charity, of course, is what the writer supports himself with while he is finishing his novel.

Hope is the virtue by which he firmly trusts that someday, somewhere, somebody will publish his novel.

But it is in the virtue of faith that the writer grounds himself (or herself) in the true religious experience of literature; and faith was defined early on for me as a firm belief in the revealed *truths*—truths of God as religion would have it; truths of the writing life, as I would have it.

"How may we sin against faith?" the catechism used to ask itself, and then it provided four answers:

Sin number 1: "By rashly accepting as truths of faith what are not really such." I take this to mean that the writer should learn how to tell the difference between literary gold and dross. Michelangelo said a work of sculpture is created by cutting away the unnecessary part of a block of marble. Georges Simenon removed all words from his work that were there just to make an effect. "You know," he said, "you have a beautiful sentence—cut it." But it was Hemingway who forever codified this issue when he said: "The most essential gift for a good writer is a built-in, shock-proof shit detector. This is the writer's radar and all great writers have had it."

Sin number 2: "By neglecting to learn the truths which we are bound to know." This is a large order. It means you should read the entire canon of literature that precedes you, back to the Greeks, up to the current issue of *The Paris Review;* and if you have any time left over, you should go out and accumulate an intimate knowledge of politics, history, language, love, philosophy, psychology, sex, madness, the underworld, soap opera, your cholesterol level, and whether the Beatles will ever have a reunion.

Sin number 3: "By not performing those acts of faith, which we are commanded to perform." This means you should write even on Christmas and your birthday, and forswear forever the excuse that you never have enough time.

Sin number 4: "By heresy and apostasy." This means writing for the movies.

You see here before you a heretic and an apostate. My life after the army was a tissue of muddle, a pilgrimage through ignorance, anxiety, and innocence, but a pilgrimage with some discernible milestones. Five years after leaving the army I would get married, write my first and last play and my twenty-fifth short story, then quit journalism to write a novel. I would write the novel and it would be awful. Seven years after the army I would become managing editor of a daily newspaper. After nine years I would quit journalism again to finish another novel. I would be showing improvement in novel writing, but not much. After fifteen years of work as a half-time journalist, half-time fictionist, I would become a movie critic. After seventeen years I would publish my first novel. After nineteen years I would become a book critic. After twenty-two years I would become a teacher. And then, after thirty-one years, I would write my first movie script, may God have mercy on my soul.

I was not always a heretic. For a time I was a true believer in journalism, lived it passionately, gained entry to worlds I had no right to enter, learned how to write reasonably well and rapidly, was never bored by what I was doing, found it an enduring source of stimulation, met thousands of the crazy people who inhabit it and learned madness from most of them. I loved the tension, the unexpected element of the news, the illusion of being at the center of things when you were really at what approximated the inner lining of the orange peel.

Also I learned who I was, in certain small but significant ways. I became, as I mentioned, a managing editor, a position to which I had been obliquely gravitating since the beginning; for in wanting to learn all there was to learn about writing, I also wanted to learn all there was about what you did with writing after you wrote it. I became an escalating figure in the editorial room: from lowly slug in the sports department, to army columnist, to inquiring reporter and rewrite man. I harangued myself onto the police beat, became Saturday city editor, feature writer, substitute night city editor, general reporter; city editor when the reigning figure went to lunch and never came back; acting managing editor when the boss infarcted myocardially. And then, at long last, managing editor.

When this happened to me—over the objection of my second self, which had always wanted to be a daily columnist until the seductive muse of fiction deflowered my pencil—I contemplated the new condition and wrote to a contemporary of mine who had also become a managing editor. He'd been a youth page writer for a local daily when I was still in college, and I always envied him that head start. Now here we were in perfect equanimity, managing editors both, he in Albany, I in Puerto Rico, and I apprised him of this, also reminding him of what Mencken had once written: "All managing editors are vermin."

I remained verminous for two years, for we had started this newspaper from scratch and it was a challenge unlike any other I'd known. I never worked harder, never found more pleasure in the work, yet always longed to be out of it, for the job had interrupted my novel in progress, and I yearned to return and see how it would turn out. It took me those two years to accumulate the courage and wisdom to quit a lucrative, fascinating job, live off my savings and a weekend editing job, and work five full days on fiction. What I had finally come to realize was that I'd learned all I wanted to learn about newspapering, and that I could never learn enough about how to write fiction; for the more I learned, the more difficult writing became; and that is still so today. I don't mean to be simplistic about journalism, which is mired in the complexity of randomness. It was a great training ground for a writer; but I'd reached my limit with it and knew in my soul that I was a committed novelist, whose work is grounded in the complexity of unconscious logic.

The problem then became the quest for the elusive Kennedy voice. I had ceased to be consciously emulative of anyone in my work, but what I was left with was what I now think of as the voice of literary objectivity, a journalistic virus, an odious microbe that paralyzes the imagination and cripples the language. "Cut, cut, cut," counsels Simenon; but what is left after all the cuts? Is there something new on the page? Something original? Is there energy in the sentence, power in the scene? In the interest of curbing excess, has the heart been cut out of the story? In the relentless quest for realistic action and surface, has the intellectual dimension been excised, or avoided?

In recent years a number of very good young writers have been, and are still being castigated, even vilified, because of the brevity of their styles and content. This is the critical assault on so-called minimalism, that word a critic's invention that is not a new subject for assaulting purposes. Forty years ago the critic Philip Rahv looked around and found the novelists of that day excluding the intellect in favor of depicting life on its physical levels (which is the journalistic way, of course). Rahv accused the American writer of "a disinclination to thought and . . . an intense predilection for the real," and found also that less gifted writers following Hemingway's method were producing "work so limited to the recording of the unmistakably real that it could be said of them that their art ended exactly where it should properly begin."

The transition from journalism to fiction is always a precarious trip, for journalism foists dangerous illusions on the incipient fiction writer. The daily journalist is trained, for instance, to forget about yesterday and focus on today. There is also a car parked downstairs, ready to carry him off into tomorrow, and so every new day becomes, for him, a tabula rasa. This is deadly. The fiction writer who puts little or no value on yesterday, or the even more distant past, might just as well have

Alzheimer's disease; for serious fiction, especially novelistic work, has time as its essence and memory as its principal tool.

The journalist is also under pressure to believe that merely his presence at the great moments—whether he be first on the scene after a murder of passion, or witness to the fall of an empire—gives him the stuff of fiction. This is true to a point, but the stuff in question is merely raw material. The writer who believes he has a ready-made work of fiction spread out before him in his notes, needful only of a bit of sprucing and spicing, is deluded. He is a victim of the cult of experience, the impulse that sends writers, who can find no value in the quotidian, off to wars and revolutions to find something to write about. More than experience is called for.

In recent months in this country we have witnessed a rather tub-thumping, hog-stomping, name-calling literary argument on this subject, begun by our contemporary, Tom Wolfe, a notable tub-thumper and baroque hog-stomper of high journalistic achievement and repute, who moved into the realm of fiction with an extraordinarily successful first novel, *Bonfire of the Vanities*. Having succeeded, he now would like others to succeed also by writing novels like his. The debate over this has flourished in the pages of *Harper's* magazine and the *New York Times Book Review,* among other places, and Mr. Wolfe has had his say twice on the subject. Also, his argument has been deconstructed by some notable figures in contemporary literature, Philip Roth, Mary Gordon, John Hawkes and Robert Towers among others, and its parts have been handed back to Mr. Wolfe, somewhat the worse for wear. Even so, there is merit in his point of view. I mentioned to him last month that I'd followed the exchange with great interest and had heard several arguments on both sides of the issue. That surprised him. "If there's anybody on my side," he said, "I haven't heard from them."

The essence of Mr. Wolfe's side of the argument is that American literature in the last half of this century has gone down the tube of privacy, inversion, neo-fabulism, magical realism, absurdism and so on, and that the only way to rescue it is through a return to realism of a nineteenth-century order, writing akin to that of Dickens, Trollope, Thackeray, Zola, and Balzac. The means of achieving this movement back to the future of the novel, says Mr. Wolfe, is reporting.

He writes: "I doubt there is a writer over forty who does not realize in his heart of hearts that literary genius, in prose, consists of proportions more on the order of 65 percent material, and 35 percent talent in the sacred crucible."

Mr. Wolfe also believes that, because of the way fiction has been written in the past twenty-five years, "Any literary person . . . will admit that in at least four years out of five the best nonfiction books have been better literature than the most highly praised books of fiction."

This latter notion has at least two memorable antecedents, one an essay by Norman Podhoretz, the editor of *Commentary* magazine, written some thirty odd years ago. As Mr. Wolfe does today, Mr. Podhoretz back then found fiction wanting in imagination, in disciplined intelligence, and also lacking a "restless interest in the life of the times."

Discursive writing, argued Mr. Podhoretz, had taken over the province that the novel had voluntarily surrendered—that province being the criticism of morals and manners. In short, the novel had no contemporary social relevance, he said, and the real art form of the age was the magazine article.

Similarly, the critic Leslie Fiedler, the great doomsayer of our era, all but exulted back in the early 1960s that the novel as a form was just about dead, that the public for novels had become sub-literate, that the artistic faith that had sustained writers was dead and, what's more, America never had an unequivocal avant-gardist among novelists of the first rank anyway.

In a sub-literate era, he wrote, who needs fiction? For, what *documentary realism* once promised to give people in *novel* form, non-fiction was providing more efficiently, more painlessly. As to the myths the sub-literates always look for—boy gets girl, good guy kills bad guy, etc.—television and film were providing them more vividly than the novel, and at less intellectual cost.

Some truth there, alas, in Mr. Fiedler's argument. Even so, it's very troublesome being a novelist when critics with a license to kill keep saying you're dead. Such complaints also cheer up *serious* people who do not find their own predilections and prejudices reflected in the novels they read. They see instead a hostile fiction that supports dangerous ideas and does not strike sufficiently critical attitudes toward the social forces and institutions that oppress certain multitudes, or certain elites. They see the literature of the age being written by the disengaged, the alienated, the untalented, the Philistines, the dropouts, the solipsists, the anarchists; and who will save us from drowning in all this irrelevance? these serious people wonder.

I could join Tom Wolfe's argument happily and point out my own black beasts of contemporary literature; but I am more inclined to defend this literature and its creators for several reasons.

What is fundamental to the counter-argument is the number of great books that have been written that did not directly concern their own time, but have prevailed as classic works nevertheless.

Consider only three of these books written out of their own age: *Benito Cereno* by Melville, written in 1856 of an event from 1797, but emblematic of the racial conflict that prevailed throughout the long era of slavery, and relevant even today; *The Red Badge of Courage* by Stephen Crane, written thirty years after the Civil War had ended, but a masterpiece of that war that speaks to all soldiers of any war; Hawthorne's first novel, *The Scarlet Letter,* written in 1850, probing the conflict between the Puritan culture of the seventeenth century and the privacy of love, but a cautionary tale of secrecy and shame whose meaning has endured, will endure.

Should we have told these writers that their choice of time was out of joint? Clearly their books are relevant not only to their own time, they are relevant to all time. I don't believe it matters whether a writer crisscrosses continents in search of today's material. I believe that what Alfred Kazin wrote is the truth: ". . . every writer criticizes life and society with every word he writes. The better the writer, the more this criticism and his imagination will fuse as one."

Or consider Tolstoy on the same subject:

> An artist's mission must not be to produce an irrefutable solution to a problem, but to compel us to love life in all its countless and inexhaustible manifestations. If I were told I might write a book in which I should demonstrate beyond any doubt the correctness of my opinions on every social problem, I should not waste two hours at it; but if I were told that what I wrote would be read twenty years from now by people who are children today, and that they would weep and laugh over my book and love life more because of it, then I should devote all my life and strength to such a work.

How can anyone have the audacity to tell a writer what and how to write? The writer, of necessity, is the sole judge of that, for the making of these decisions is evolutionary, a process of trial and rejection, of finally choosing among infinite possibilities the method, and story, and characters that allow the work to be written at all. I could never fault any writer for not writing about the age, for in my own experience it has been extremely difficult; and I offer only one example.

My time in the army represented two years of my life, and not merely life lived, but life reported on through a newsman's eye—reporting on the army, on Germany, on the cold war getting hot, on an innocent abroad, on fraternization with frauleins, on the black market, on army skulduggery, on leftover Naziism, and much more. I had, and still have some of that world at my fingertips; and also I've gone back twice to Germany to rekindle my memory.

Why? Well I wanted to write about it all, and did write about it—in short stories over a decade; and all those stories died. I also wrote about two hundred pages of a novel about it, and that too died. Why do my stories die when clearly I have at least 65 percent of them living right there in the file cabinet? Obviously, in my case, because it is not the *material* that makes a work of fiction come to life. It is, in fact, almost impossible to say what it is that does that. Material can begin a piece of work, emotion and ideas can keep it going, but in order for the work not to self-destruct along the way, something else must happen. The writer must find himself in a strange place full of unknowns, populated by characters who are not quite strangers but about whom little is certain, everything is to be discovered. There must be a transformation of the material, of the characters, of the age, into something that is intriguingly new to the writer. "Art," wrote Boris Pasternak, "is interested in life at the moment when the ray of power is passing through it."

The writer, when he is functioning as an artist, understands when this power is at hand, and he knows that it does not rise up from his note-pad but up from the deepest part of his unconscious, which knows everything everywhere and always: that secret archive stored in the soul at birth, enhanced by every waking moment of life, and which is the source of the power and the vision that allows the writer to create something never before heard or seen on earth.

This creation of the new is what a good reader seeks and will recognize. Listen to Seamus Heaney, for instance, on what he expects from good poetry: "You want it to touch you at the melting point below the breastbone and the beginning of the solar plexus. You want something sweetening and at the same time something unexpected, something that has come through constraint into felicity."

Or E. M. Forster trying to define *Moby Dick*. He calls the book a yarn about whaling interspersed with snatches of poetry, also a battle against evil conducted too long or in the wrong way, also a contest between two unreconciled evils; and then he throws up his hands: "These are words," says Forster, "a symbol for the book if we want one, but . . . the essential in *Moby Dick is* prophetic song, which flows athwart the action and the surface morality like an undercurrent. It lies outside words."

Prophetic song. Nice work if you can get it.

Almost, but not quite, just by the nature of Melville's effort, one might conclude he was striving for that song from the outset. But to think that is to believe in creation as nothing more than conception; that the song, the achievement, was already present in the embryo. If this were true, what then can we say of Melville's years of gestation among whales, his months of research ("I have swam through libraries," his narrator writes in *Moby Dick,* and the same was true of Melville) and his year and a half of writing and rewriting the text? One of his biographers pointed out that although seventeen months seems a short time for the composition of such a book, it would have been an unusually *long* period given the manic pace at which Melville was writing.

An ancillary note: Nathaniel Hawthorne, with whom Melville became soul-mates during the writing of *Moby Dick,* had taken ten years for his own literary embryo to mature into the form and substance that became *The Scarlet Letter.*

Writers (and their songs) grow like plants, like trees, like children, like disease, like love. They go through stages of fragility, woodenness, pubescence, death, and passion. You'll note that I have put death before passion. This corresponds to the crucifixion, burial, descent into hell, and resurrection that befalls all literary careerists who keep the faith. Fitzgerald's noted line, "There are no second acts in American lives," was cockeyed and trivializing. He was talking about stardom. Resurrection has come to many American writers—Melville, the most egregiously belated case, and Faulkner, and Henry James, and Kate Chopin and Willa Cather, and Edith Wharton, and Fitzgerald himself, (though he was dead at the time); and it is now happening with Hemingway. It even happened to Faulkner when he was still alive, the problem being that no one knew he was alive, his books all out of print. Then suddenly they were *in* print and still are, along with those of the other writers in this group, who have all been elevated to a cosmic status that will long outlast the stars as Fitzgerald perceived them.

Not all of these writers wrote of their own age, though most did; and most of them were realists; but not Melville, and not always James, who wrote romances and took excursions into the world of ghosts. In the words of Maupassant, they each made themselves "an illusion of a world," each according to his or her sex, knowledge, style, talent, joyful or melancholy disposition, mythic or mordant mind.

So whose realism is this anyway?

And what of dreams? Are they part of realism?

And what of the surrealistic episodes that all of us have gone through but try not to accept as real? Kafka and Borges and García Márquez have made them real, without doubt, just as they were supposed to; because they found it necessary. "The great artists," said Maupassant, "are those who impose their particular illusion on humanity."

I am delighted to report to you that pursuing my own particular illusion I have just finished a section of a new novel in which I use—at long last—that experience I had in Germany so many years ago. I am also pleased to report that I have transformed it to such a degree that it no longer resembles anything I lived through. The character who inhabits this transformed experience is forever doing things that are wild and illegal and outrageous; not at all like me, which may be the reason I could never before write about the place. Yes. Absolutely. That last possibility is so clearly accurate that I hereby aver its truth: that I couldn't write it *because* I had lived it; because I knew it *too well;* because I knew *how it would come out:* boringly, as it always had.

The writer usually feels that any successful transformation of the work is a form of personal growth; but also that he's transformed his chosen art form, the novel, a micromillimeter or two, as well. Mr. Fiedler and other undertakers who have come after him, tend to think otherwise. As the novel replaced narrative poetry as the reigning form, so the movies and television will replace the novel, is their view. Since the form of the novel no longer progresses, they argue, since it doesn't redefine itself beyond what the modernists—Joyce, Proust, Mann, etc.—were able to do, then it is doomed to repeat itself, grow moldy, and become an esoteric genre only antiquarians will pursue henceforth.

Maybe it is all too true that the attention span of the reading audience is now at the level of a manic Siamese cat, and that the future of the word lies with magazine journalists and screenwriters; but I don't buy it. I've worked in those usurping forms and will work in them again. I love them both. But I live for the novel and will never believe it is less than what Henry James called it—the great form, in which *anything* is possible.

Back in the late 1950s, when I was trying to read the complete shelf of William Faulkner, I kept coming across speeches or interviews in which he talked of uplifting man's heart. In his Nobel speech he said it was the writer's "privilege to help man endure by lifting his heart." In a literature class at the University of Virginia he said: ". . . the artist believes what he's doing is valid in that it may do something to uplift man's heart, not to make man any more successful, but to temporarily make him feel better than he felt before, to uplift his heart for a moment."

This uplift business baffled me. I was reading and re-reading *The Sound and The Fury* and *Sanctuary* and *Light in August* and *The Wild Palms* and *Absalom Absalom*—tales of incest and whoring and rape and dying love and madness and murder and racial hate and miscegenational tragedy and idiocy—and saying to myself, "This is uplift?"

But I kept reading and found I couldn't get enough; had to reread to satisfy the craving, and came to answer the question in a word: yes. I felt exalted by the man's work, not by reveling in all the disasters, but learning from his language and his insights, and his storytelling genius, how certain other people lived and thought. I was privileged to enter into the most private domains of their lives and they became my friends, or people I'd keep at least at arm's length, or people I pitied, or feared, or loved. This was truly an uplifting experience, something akin to real friendship, and I began to understand the process by which writing reaches into another person's heart.

Now let me mention two letters I received from a man who had read my novel *Ironweed.* About four years ago he wrote the first letter. He was moved by the book and had to write and tell me. Two years later came the second letter in which he hinted he might have known the street life, the drinking life of a bum, just as *Ironweed's* hero, Francis Phelan, knew it. The letter writer was now living with his sister, doing handyman's work for her, and staying out of trouble. His sister didn't like drunks, and would even cross the street to get away from a wino. Then her brother pressed *Ironweed* on her, got her to watch a home video of the film of it, and got her to read the book. At the end she found herself crying, and she said to her brother, about Francis, "You know, he wasn't such a bad guy."

That would be quite enough for me, but the story has a coda. The sister no longer fears winos, no longer crosses the street to get away from them. She now gives them her loose change. And at Christmas she passes out to them, one and all, half-pints of muscatel.

This is a true story. It is a realistic story of our age. It has been transformed somewhat by the writer, who is very glad to have written it.

Families and Prisons

Robert Hass

I had in mind for today an odd and very particular subject—I wanted to speak about some of the emotions that arose from the representation of family relationships in recent poetry, or perhaps I should say autobiographical representations of family in recent American lyric poetry. And that talk might have been called, if it were going to be a straightforward historical investigation of the subject, Poor Monkeys and the White Business in the Trees. I can think of lots of reasons for not talking about this subject—one of them is that "subject" never seems to be a very fruitful approach to poetry—so let me mention some reasons for doing so.

One is that there is so much autobiographical poetry about families, and another is the fact that, in the history of lyric poetry, it is such a new subject. Which is surprising when you consider that family is one of the fundamental subjects of literature. Almost all the great Greek tragedies are about families, and so are many of the great novels of the nineteenth century. The greatest American play of the twentieth century is about family—take your choice among the ones worth reading, *A Long Day's Journey Into Night, Death of a Salesman, The Glass Menagerie,* A *Streetcar Named Desire.* Even *Who's Afraid of Virginia Woolf* is about family rather than a couple, because an imagined child is at the center of that play. And the best American novel of the twentieth century—here you choose, I suppose, between *The Sound and the Fury* and *Absalom! Absalom!*— is about family. And yet before the appearance of Robert Lowell's *Life Studies* and Allen Ginsberg's *Kaddish,* it's hard to think of serious work in poetry that touches on the subject, even though it has, in the last thirty years, become fundamental, as commonplace and omnipresent a subject as erotic love was in the sixteenth century, or man's relationship to God in the seventeenth. American students of literature are likely to know something about Allen Ginsberg's Aunt Rose or Elizabeth Bishop's Aunt Consuelo, but it is a fact that they would

---

The Hopwood Lecture, 1991

learn nothing from the body of past literature about the aunts or grandmothers of John Donne, Thomas Traherne, Anne Finch, Alexander Pope, Samuel Johnson, Thomas Gray, Emily Dickinson, or Robert Browning.

It's also the case that it is an almost exclusively American subject. American poetry is full of aunts and grandmothers, but French poetry isn't, or Serbian poetry, or Arabic or Brazilian or, for that matter, English poetry. Part of the explanation for this is surely that the autobiographical and personal stance in American poetry has not asserted itself in the same way in other literatures. It really does seem to have to do with American culture and American mores. It may possibly have to do with the fact that class is a somewhat less explosive subject in American society than in most other literate societies. It may be that it's a little easier to talk about family without seeming either to be bragging or complaining. I remember, a few years ago, hearing an American poet who has tried to write seriously about politics quoting with some relief and approval a Peruvian poet who said he had no stomach for Americans and their little, personal poems. Another version of this reaction comes from a Czech poet who is supposed to have said of an American woman writing in the autobiographical mode, "That's not poetry; it's gynecology." Like the original scandal of Walt Whitman's "Song of Myself," the implicit and explicit self-absorption of much of this poetry remains—not for American culture at large which in this case shares and mirrors the preoccupation of the poets, but for international intellectual culture—a scandal.

Still it's not autobiography that I'm concerned with, but the subject of family in autobiography. What distinguishes writing about family from writing about other relationships is the presence, I think, of the idea of the child. Even a poem dealing with two adult sisters is *about* childhood because a shared childhood is implied. Which is why one term of this talk might have been Poor Monkey. It's the title of a study of childhood in literature by an English scholar, Peter Coveney. The phrase comes from Shakespeare's *Richard III.* Young children rarely show up in the art of the Renaissance, and so we get a glimpse, a bare glimpse, of the feeling that attached to them in the one phrase uttered upon the news that the two boy princes have been murdered in the Tower. "Poor monkeys," their mother says.

The pathos and tenderness in that phrase are among the emotions called up in literature by familial feeling that interest me. Another is rage, and all the buried forms that that emotion can take. I should say that my thinking about these feelings isn't disinterested. I've written in the past about family life from the point of view of a parent. I have lately been trying with some difficulty to write—I don't know if "about" is the preposition I want; perhaps "in" or "with"—some of my childhood experiences. In my early childhood my mother was chronically alcoholic which filled my days, or some of them, with instability, sorrow, and some terror. Also, and more problematic for a writer, a certain amount of amnesia. This is the context which led me to this subject and also the cause of a certain mild suspicion I have of my own motives for wanting to talk about it. So I have practical reasons for trying to understand why one's childhood is available as a subject, what it means that others have written about it in the way that they have at this point in history, what problems are implicit in the techniques and what are implicit in the subject. Another of my motives must very likely be to justify myself.

Let me say a quick series of thoughts about the first subject because I want to turn now to the second.

—The subject of the child enters literature with romanticism, which is also to say that it enters literature when the middle class becomes its main creator and audience;

—So its appearance is connected to most of the propositions of romanticism—subjectivity, radical freedom, radical inwardness, sincerity, visionary innocence, transparency of language, realism as a mode of representation;

—So it is also connected to romantic political thought; that is, the child emerges not long after the idea of the rights of man emerged; the kind of political feeling that descends to us through Blake, Dickens, Hugo, Dostoevsky, Chekhov braided together our feelings about the abuse of power and the abuse of children; *Oliver Twist* can stand for this, or *Les Misérables;*

—An even more brutal simplification: romanticism invented psychoanalysis which has, if not shaped, deeply colored our way of thinking about the child, the family, and the human person;

—The child actually appears in English literature in the latter part of the eighteenth century in what is often called the age of sensibility, at the same time as work associated with the development of the Gothic novel, and the literature of sentiment, and the theory of the sublime; it has had this association with tears and terror, sentimentality and awe; so there is always this suspect sentimental side to the subject;

—The literature of sentimentality emerged when the middle class emerged and when mercantile imperialism was well underway; the child emerged in literature—Blake saw this in a flash and so in his way did Dickens—shadowed by a dark, unhappy child who was elsewhere.

These observations, hunches, are drawn from a sense of the history of literature; what their active use to a writer is I'm not sure. There are other kinds of observation to draw on as well. That feeling of pathos, the lump-in-the-throat feeling that shows up in movies about families like *Kramer vs. Kramer,* is at least one of the elements of an actual social bond, of a particular imagination of civility, morality. Tears in a movie theater: some part of one's mind always feels immersed in this sea of tender, bruised feeling with its heavy tidal surgings and withdrawals, and some part of many of us—Oscar Wilde on Dickens' Little Nell—is made uneasy, demurs. A few years ago in a divorce court I saw a young woman sitting in the courtroom, well-dressed, back straight, ignoring the proceedings and reading a book with a title like *How to Survive Unspeakable Psychological Pain.* Outside in the corridor there was a young man in a baggy suit sitting on the polished oak bench, bent over a lap computer, intently performing what looked like complicated equations: the husband. It seemed funny and perhaps sad, and then when one instinctively thought that there were children involved, probably two, probably under eight, being kept for the day by the wife's sister, a different emotion qualified the scene. You see what interests me about this. Families are built around a core of very painful wishing. It's palpable in the atmosphere of the world we live in.

One more element in this survey, a more writerly consideration. I have been reading an extraordinarily interesting critical book by Wendy Lesser called *His Other Half.* It's about male artists writing about women, and in a chapter about writers who write about their mothers, she remarks that we are always in such work in the presence of a split subject, of a division between the point of view of the adult writer and the point of view of the child self. And, of course, she points out, that child self is irrecoverable, it can only be approximated in language, the way the taste of a pear can only be approximated, or something seen in the street. As for the adult self, every word one writes issues from it presumably, but if one turns one's attention to it directly one sees that it is also unknowable. It's busy creating itself, and when it interrogates the child-self in that process—did this really happen? is this how it was?—it gets no answer. That's how the literary history comes to be important. The gaps in the act of writing where the unknowable and irrecoverable occur are rarely empty; one's unconsciously absorbed sense of the territory, in the form of genre, ideas, emotions, even phrases, rushes in to fill that void. It's how tradition actually works on the individual talent and it's why literature most often reproduces literature.

I will come back to this subject, but I want to turn now to the matter of self-justification, because when I began to think about this lecture, it was this that made me, for a good while, tongue-tied. A French poet—I think it was Reverdy—has said that all talk about poetics is more or less indiscreet praise of one's own method. And this is no doubt true, but it is only partly true. Let's say the first two-thirds of any lecture on poetry by a poet is likely to be more or less indiscreet self-praise; the final third is apt to deal with the supreme importance of poetry to human civilization.

The Polish novelist Witold Gombrowicz has written a very sensible essay—you can find it in his diaries published in English translation by Northwestern University Press—in which he argues that the proof of the greatness of poetry as an art is the fact that, though no one wants to read it or think about it, though it bores people to tears, and almost no one would under any circumstance short of compulsion read a long poem, and would only in moments of weakmindedness have the thought that it would occasionally be a good idea to read short ones, a thought which, by the way, they scarcely ever yield to, if they do have it,—though this is the case, Gombrowicz argues, and everyone acknowledges it is the case if they bother to think about it at all, poets have nevertheless by the sheer brute tactic of talking endlessly and on all possible occasions from the beginning of human utterance to the present moment about the truth, beauty, daring, wisdom, depths, sublimity, fineness, strength, power, necessity and indispensable force of poetry, that everyone else, mainly because the noise has been so incessant and they have had too many other actual concerns pressing upon them to bring the matter to the center of their minds, has more or less yielded, at least as a piety, to this barrage of propaganda from the poets and conceded to poetry the poets' idea of its value.

If you doubt the Gombrowicz thesis, you have only to consult a published volume of previous Hopwood lectures and read one delivered by a poet, the lecture, for example, that the English poet Donald Davie—with whom I had the good luck to study briefly—gave in 1965, which ends, "The prophet exists on sufferance, he is society's expense account, part of what society can sometimes afford. Not so the poet; he is what society cannot dispense with." And there is Denise Levertov's lecture in 1968. "Reverence for life," she says, "if it is a necessary relationship to the world must be so for all people, not only for poets. Yes: but it is the poet who has language in his care; the poet who more than others recognizes language also as a *form of life* and a common resource to be cherished and served as we should serve and cherish earth and its waters, animal and vegetable life, and each other."

W. D. Snodgrass in 1974 almost avoided the issue by simply giving a wonderful lecture on *A Midsummer Night's Dream,* but he did stop at one point in the proceedings to ask a question. "Who says poetry makes nothing happen?" In fact, W. H. Auden said it in an elegy for W. B. Yeats, poets' elegies for each other being one of the main forms of their insistent chorus of self-praise and self-reference. Snodgrass doesn't answer his own question because quoting what sounds like poetry and acting as if the audience is familiar with the source is another of the main tactics of poets. The art is called allusion; whether Snodgrass was discreetly alluding to a tradition of great poets who deployed themselves publicly in a pair of initials beginning with "W." I can't say. He continues: "The artist's open rendering of his emotions may have such unpredictable effects on the public that totalitarians from Plato to Stalin have been willing (with some justice) to muzzle or exterminate these unacknowledged and unconscious legislators." Notice that Snodgrass might have characterized poetry in various ways, but that he describes it as having to do with "the artist's open rendering of his emotions." Snodgrass was especially thought of in 1974 as one of the initiators of what was called "confessional poetry," so his definition of the danger of art is what Reverdy meant, though his aim in this particular passage is not to praise himself, but to assert the importance of poetry in general.

And notice that, about Stalin, Snodgrass was absolutely right. He had Osip Mandelstam and Isaac Babel exterminated, just as Lenin had Nikolai Gumilev exterminated, who died before a firing squad—in a gesture that Gombrowicz would have found completely typical of the self-importance of poets as a breed—with a volume of Homer clutched to his breast. There are poets in jail in the Republic of Korea right now, and it is at least arguable that our tax money helped to put them there. There are poets in jail in Iraq and Syria and it seems likely that before long there will be poets in the prisons of Kuwait. But of course it's possible for Gombrowicz to argue that these poets are the victims of their own success, and that the only reason they are in jail is that they have succeeded in deluding their rulers into the conception of their importance that put them there.

It is a complicated matter, thinking about poets in prison, once you have said that they shouldn't be there and that civilized people should be doing something in their lives to get them, and all other political prisoners, out. One of the Korean poets who was in jail in 1986 when I was in Seoul to participate in an international conference of writers on the freedom to write was a young man named Kim Nam Ju. Last name: Kim, as Korean custom is, first names Nam Ju. Kim Nam Ju had been in prison for three years, was permitted the use of writing materials for an hour once a month, was reported to have blood in his urine and no access to a doctor. The Korean government allowed members of our group to visit him and spoke in general terms of forthcoming amnesties as the process of democratization and reconciliation progressed, but they did not release him from jail and there were intense discussions among the visiting writers about whether it was appropriate to attend lavish banquets sponsored by Samsung and Hyundai while some of their colleagues were imprisoned by the government that regulates the country in the interests of these corporations. The argument had basically to do with whether we would do the writers more good by being polite to our hosts or rude to our hosts. Perhaps to sharpen the issue the imprisoned writers announced a hunger strike. In the end the Americans, West Germans, Poles, Swedes, Danes, and Norwegians boycotted the banquets. Everyone else attended; the French, English, Japanese, Yugoslavian, and Canadian delegations were particularly eloquent on the subject of diplomacy and scornful of what they called moral showing-off.

It was interesting to see writers from all over the world lobbying each other, in the corridors of a hotel named after an American general, about whether it was better to kiss the dictator's hand or not kiss the dictator's hand in order to get their colleagues out of prison. It was an argument, I suppose, that had to occur. And afterwards some of the poets sat down in the hotel to feasts of *bulgoki* and fresh fish and fowl, pungent with the odor of Korean spices, chili and pickled cabbage. A Russian poet who has taken political risks in his life sat down to those meals and so did a very good Japanese novelist known for his tormented conscience. The others, the dissenters, went out to dinner instead. One has to eat, and they ate in alleyway restaurants where the fish was so fresh the waiters brought to the table as a first course pieces of the tentacles of octopus, carefully cut and still squirming.

I did not get much of a sense of the poetry of Kim Nam Ju. It was, of course, unavailable. The few poems I did see were unpublished English translations of what seemed like youthful work. There was a description of a field, I remember, seen from a prison train, a sense of homesickness. Another poet who was in jail was named Lee Tae Bok. ("Lee" is pronounced "Yee.") He had been imprisoned for a violation of the publishing law because he'd printed a book-length poem about a farmer's revolt in 1947 on an island on the southern tip of Korea. It was a sensitive subject. Korea, as you know, was occupied by the Japanese from 1905 to 1945 and no society is ruled by an invading power for that long without a lot of collaboration and bad conscience. Lee Tae Bok was also young, twenty-three or twenty-four. I helped translate the peroration of his long poem, working in a hotel room between convention sessions with a very brave and intelligent Korean poet. "And so," it began, as I recall, "the authorities who were the running dogs of Japanese imperialism / changed their uniforms and became the running dogs of American imperialism / I write this down in 1986 when the blood of Korea cries out / and the tears of Korea burst forth." The language of the literal translation sounded to me like the slogans one saw on the banners at student demonstrations. My co-translator had expressed no opinion about the quality of the poem. I asked him if its language was interesting in Korean. He smiled at me, nodding, as if he had an amused, distant recollection of that state of mind in which one might ask such a question, and then shrugged and said that the language had a certain vigor.

When I was in Yugoslavia in 1982, the poet who was in jail in Belgrade was named Goyko Djogo. He writes in Serbian, and he came from a peasant family, I was told, in Bosnia-Herzegovina, and, because of his background, he had been especially encouraged. His first book was published when he was quite young. His second book was approved for publication; by then he lived in Belgrade, but when it appeared in print there was a line in one poem which had not been in the approved manuscript. It was a nightmarish poem and it ended with a line about "a one-armed monster in Liberation Square." Serbian poetry is surreal, but everyone knew that Marshall Tito had lost an arm in World War II, and Djogo went to jail. I know a Cuban poet who was in prison for seven years, was released on several conditions including his refraining from reading his poems in public. He immediately read his poems in public and went back to jail for, I think, five more years. His poems, I am sorry to say, are terrible. There is fairly wide agreement among people competent to judge about this point. His story belongs to the history of courage, rather than to the history of literature.

I'll tell you a story which may or may not be true because it belongs to the history of marvels. The French poet Robert Desnos was in Buchenwald; he had been arrested for his activities in the Resistance. The story is that Desnos and all the men in his barracks were marched to a room and told to strip in preparation for being deloused in an adjoining room. They understood what that meant, and Desnos turned to the man next to him and said, "I read fortunes. Let me see your palm." The man, stoop-shouldered, eyes wet with fear, held up his palm. Desnos looked at it and shook his head. A long life-line, he said, but I see trouble in business down the line and trouble with your daughter. The man, stunned at first, laughed. And others laughed. And soon all the men in the room were standing around naked, laughing, with tears in their eyes, reading one another's palms. The guards were so disconcerted that they ordered the men to get dressed and marched them back to their barracks. The next day a transfer order came through and many were sent to a work camp and some survived to tell this story. Desnos was not among the survivors. Surrealism began with the idea that freedom of imagination could transform life, and in this instance, if the story is true, it did.

Many of you must know by now the story of the Russian poet Irina Ratushinskaya, who composed her poems in prison sometimes by scratching them with a matchstick on a bar of soap. It is a story people like to tell and it has crossed my mind to wonder if it would have made any difference in the telling if the poems were mediocre, heartfelt and full of clichés. Tadeusz Borowski, the Polish writer who wrote the brilliant and terrible stories about Auschwitz published under the title *This Way to the Gas Chambers, Ladies and Gentlemen,* also wrote poetry when he was in the concentration camp and what interested me about it was how conventional it was. The moonlight in the barracks was "ghostly," the sheets were "lambent," the silence "deep." And so on—it seems the lines could have been written by any undergraduate about his dormitory room. And later, after the war, in a d.p. camp in Germany, having survived the inferno and witnessed its workings, he wrote bitter poems against the new order he saw emerging in the Occupation. The symbol of this order in the poems is ugly, laughing, black American G.I.s consorting with blonde women in the cafes of Berlin. There are not many of these images in the poems—perhaps three or four—but they are enough to demonstrate that the experience of Auschwitz doesn't necessarily cure racism.

Which brings us to another famously imprisoned poet—Ezra Pound. And to an interesting question. If an American poet—perhaps she developed an interest in Sufi mysticism—was living in Baghdad, was pro-Palestinian, knew a little Arabic, had translated poets of the Taf'ila Movement in Iraq, and, having been treated well by the Baathist government, believed in Saddam Hussein's anticlerical, anti-communist approach to Arab socialism and even wrote a little book published by a small press back in the States comparing Saddam Hussein to Thomas Jefferson, describing him as a sane, tough-minded, disciplined and visionary politician, if this woman—how could she be so stupid?—had during the recent war made radio broadcasts from Baghdad denouncing the war and Bush and the oil companies and the coalition, would she have been guilty of treason? Should she have been locked up in a facility in Basra and brought to Washington, charged with her crime, allowed to plead insanity to save herself from hanging, and be put into a relatively pleasant mental hospital (of course, this assumes that the government still maintained such institutions, had not yet discovered the therapeutic benefits of the streets) for ten years or so? Pound, after all, was not arrested for the anti-Semitic poison that seeped from him in the Rome broadcasts and for which I think I have always vaguely imagined he was punished and deserved to be punished; he was charged with betraying his country because he didn't like the war and was on the other side. It is quite possible to argue that he should not have been, and to add the United States to the list of countries that imprisoned its poets.

And there are more stories, the brave and rather old-fashioned Hungarian poet Tibor Tollas in 1956 reading the English poet Thomas Hood in a jail cell and pacing to his rhythms, the very good Hungarian poet Miklos Radnóti dead in the camps, the Peruvian poet César Vallejo imprisoned for political activity, the Greek poet Yannis Ritsos for communism, the Turkish poet Nazim Hikmet for communism, and, finally, indelibly, the Russian poet Osip Mandelstam for anti-communism.

If we tell these stories, if we mention the great poets and the poor ones, if we recall them in some detail, Mandelstam jumping from the window of a psychiatric hospital to try to kill himself, writing odes praising Stalin to try to save his skin, hounded from town to town with his wife, writing those stinging last poems; the family of Kim Nam Ju getting up subscription dinners in lower middle-class restaurants in Seoul to finance a petition for their son's release; Pound writing poems about angels and light in St. Elizabeth's while taking a lively interest in the John Birch Society; the untalented Cuban poet reading novels aloud to his illiterate cellmates; they look more and more like the spectacle of human life, and less and less like the special distinction of poetry.

Not that heroism and the task of witness have not fallen to poets as they have fallen to others, but that, when we survey the scenes evoked by W. D. Snodgrass, we see that this heroic circumstance is mysteriously like everything else—that some poets with a great gift might lack courage and some with the courage might lack the gift, that some were steadfast, some faltered, some were duplicitous and redeemed themselves, some were pure victims, helpless as crickets in a cage, and some were wrong, and did harm. A few of their stories belong to the history of literature, some to the history of contrariness, valor, cowardice, to tragedy, and to loss so sickening and pointless it is not tragic.

I have found myself thinking often about the figure of Mandelstam—or rather about people thinking about the figure of Mandelstam. There is hardly a poet alive, it seems, who has not written a poem about him. Since most of us know his difficult poems mostly in translation, this strength of feeling about him is to some extent a tribute to his wife's art—to the power of her portrait of him—rather than to the poems themselves. He is a tremendously moving figure. But I am made uneasy by our fascination with him for a couple of reasons. The first is that I think Gombrowicz might be right to suspect that our fascination exists because his martyrdom flatters us. One stubborn poet hunted to death like a wild animal by the organized violence—the *intellectual* violence as well as the police power—of the state. It is a compelling image in this century. But what I fear is that in our admiration for this image there is a confusion between the task of poetry when it finds the burning coal of history has been pressed to its lips and the task of poetry in general. The danger of this is that there is something wrong with admiring the calamitous. Also to mistake the power of poetry in our need to praise it. Writers like everyone else need examples to teach them courage and responsibility—Akhmatova waiting outside the prison wall in Moscow for news of her son, Whitman in the hospital wards of the Civil War, Ai Qing nursing the socket of his blinded eye in the wake of an attack by young Red Guards and continuing to work on his poems—but poetry needs to be able as well to face toward the world when no one's suffering gives it special drama.

Let me read you a fragment of a poem that haunts me when I think about this subject. It was written by Czeslaw Milosz in 1943 during the Nazi occupation of Warsaw. The poem is called "The Songs of Adrian Zelinski." Milosz used the figure of Zelinski to write poems which do not rise to the occasion of history, that are spoken by someone who simply feels cursed at having to live in an ugly, dangerous time and place. Zelinski mostly doesn't think about others; he just feels sorry for himself. I'll read you a little of a translation of the beginning of the poem to give you the flavor of it:

> *The fifth spring of war is beginning.*
> *A young girl is weeping for her lover.*
> *Snow is melting in the Warsaw streets.*
>
> I thought my youth would last forever,
> That I would always be the same.
> And what remains? Fear in the early hours,
> I peer at myself as at a plaque of blank, gray stone,
>
> *A carousel drones in the little square.*
> *Somebody is shooting at somebody out there.*
> *A light squall blows from the torpid river.*
>
> But what is all that to me?
> I'm like a child who can't tell a dandelion
> From a star. This isn't the wisdom
> That I bargained for. What are centuries,
> What is history? I hack out each day
> And it's a century to me.
>
> O Lord, throw me a tiny plume of pity.

The passage I had in mind occurs in the middle of the poem, where Adrian Zelinski imagines an elsewhere:

> Somewhere there are happy cities.
> Somewhere there are, but not for certain.
> Where, between the market and the sea,
> In a spray of sea mist,
> June pours wet vegetables from baskets

And ice is carried to a terrace cafe
Sprinkled with sunlight, and flowers
Drop onto women's hair.

The ink of newspapers new every hour.
Disputes about what is good for the republic.
The teeming cinemas smell of orange peels
And a mandolin hums long into the night.
Before sunrise a bird flicking the dew of song.
Somewhere there are happy cities
But they are of no use to me.
I look into life and death as into an empty winecup.
Glittering buildings or a rout of ruins.
Let me go away in peace.
A whisper of night breathes in me.

They are dragging a guy by his stupid legs,
The calves in silk socks,
The head trailing behind.
And a stain in the sand a month of rain won't wash away.
Children with toy automatic pistols
Take a look, resume their play.

To see this, or to enter an almond orchard,
Or to stand with a guitar at a sculpted gate.
Let me go away in peace.
This is not the same; possibly, it is the same.

"But not for certain" is probably the key phrase. Still, I had the sensation the first time I read this poem that Adrian Zelinski was peering into a mirror at us, while we, living in a space cleared of political violence, deprivation, censorship, peered back through the mirror at him, with fascination, and perhaps even a certain secret envy. If there are happy cities, we live in them. And though they are full of violence and deprivation and are partly supported, most of us suspect or think we know, by the export of violence and deprivation, and of censorship which we then send out our writers on cultural tours to denounce, and though one tries to acknowledge all of this and to specify that "we" in this case means most people in western Europe and the United States who read and write books, and not everyone, nevertheless it is true that the cities we live in are, with their newspapers, oranges, roads without barricades, careers, flower stalls, lectures on the condition of the culture daringly exposing its ideological biases, plus movies, plus late-night cafes with music, more or less the places Adrian Zelinski had in mind.

And in those cities, at least in the American ones, the poets have been writing poems about families. It's perhaps useful to distinguish between poems about the families the writers are living in and poems about the families they came from. Because the poems about current family life tend, in one way or another, to be about hope, and the poems about the past, often much darker, tend to be about fate. Not all poets have written these poems, of course. Some seem to have avoided the subject assiduously and others to be, simply, not interested. But the subject is everywhere. There is John Berryman's preoccupation with his father's suicide, Robert Lowell's meticulous, affectionate, and contemptuous (as I read it) catalogue of the articles in his father's room, Sylvia Plath's rage at her father, C. K. Williams's admiration for his mother for having the sensitivity and strength to stop moving her lips when he talked, Robert Pinsky's equally complicated settling of accounts with his mother in "History of My Heart," Sharon Olds's funny, terrible, hyperbolic account of the punishments parents inflicted on well-brought-up children in the nineteen fifties, Frank Bidart's philosophical despair at his inability to speak meaningfully with his mother, Gary Snyder's account of bathing with his family, Anne Sexton's poems to her daughters. Even poets who are leery of subject matter like Michael Palmer in *First Figure* and Lyn Hejenian in *My Life* find themselves working in a language constituted by an idea of family. The list could go on for a very long time.

I can't say that I understand why. Certainly what it looked like at the time was a reaction against the doctrine of impersonality in high modernism, especially in the ideas and practice of T. S. Eliot. At the time there was a sense of masks being ripped off. There are various accounts of the chronology. In one of them W. D. Snodgrass was a student of Robert Lowell's at Iowa where he wrote "Heart's Needle," a suite of what seemed then extremely personal poems about a divorce. Lowell, whose work was changing, was given a clue from his student for the work in *Life Studies*. He in turn taught Sylvia Plath and Anne Sexton in a night class in Boston and they borrowed the autobiographical mode from their teacher, and John Berryman, looking on, learned the lesson from his friends. Allen Ginsberg's evolution was independent, but he took part of his lesson from Whitman. Perhaps it's hard to remember now what Ginsberg meant when he called Whitman in "A Supermarket in California" a "lonely old courage-teacher." It was only a few years earlier that the young Robert Duncan had had a poem accepted at the *Kenyon Review* by Lowell's teacher, John Crowe Ransom, only to have it returned when Ransom saw an essay by Duncan (this was 1948) proposing the idea of civil rights for homosexuals. Ransom said he didn't mind Duncan's sexual preference, he minded him advertising it. In this context "Howl" and "America" with its memorable patriotic ejaculation, "America I'm putting my queer shoulder to the wheel" were as crucial to the sense of tossing out the theory of impersonality as the personal poems of Lowell and Sexton and Plath.

But this account is deceptive, because in another way the example of Eliot, and Yeats, and Pound, *was* autobiographical. Everyone who read "The Waste Land" understood that it was among other things the account of a personal crisis. And so while scholars read the footnotes and tracked down the references and studied Eliot's ruminations on the prospects of Christendom, the young poets understood that both the power and the immense prestige of the poem lay in its sense of personal extremity and in its identification of that personal crisis, the terrible sense of sexual unhappiness and impending madness and exile from a father's authority, with the predicament of Western civilization. The lesson of Eliot for young writers was that their most intimate suffering was a powerful metaphor, and the obvious step in the evolution of modern poetry was to speak about that suffering directly.

The first name given to this upwelling was, as you know, "confessional poetry." It is, in the end, an unfortunate name, but at the time it made for a useful confusion. If you read "confessional" in a Catholic sense, it implied a model of poetry in which the poets made forms that both confessed and somehow transformed or expiated their pain. That idea brought the wildness of the content of some of the poems into a traditional context; it connected it notionally to metaphysical poetry and the Anglo-Catholicism of Eliot and the recently shed Roman Catholicism of Lowell. It connected it in this way to a dominant and conservative literary tradition. And if you took "confession" in a Protestant sense, or even in the sense that popular magazines gave it, some sense of personal witness or ecstatic blurting or rebirth from sin to the inner light was implied, which would have suited Allen Ginsberg as an account of it and connected the work to the visionary lineage in Romantic poetry. And these differences made a difference at the level of language because Lowell was very much interested in poaching on the territory of fiction; he was interested in social detail, in the psychology of objects and people, in social class; he had Chekhov and Faulkner in mind as much as any poet, whereas Ginsberg was interested in William Carlos Williams and Blake and the kind of modernism that hadn't taken in America, surrealism,

The term "confessional" was not particularly helpful with this. It emphasized the sensational aspect of the new writing. It is odd from our present perspective to look back just those few years and see that some of the work of Sexton and Plath got called confessional because it was about the physical experiences of women. What got masked by this account of the unmasking was the obvious fact that a new autobiographical writing had emerged from modernism, and that much of the new writing was about intimate and ordinary materials of life that had not before found their way into lyric poetry, and that both the values of transparency and sincerity that the autobiographical materials implied and that had been complicated terrifically by the practice of modernism and the visionary, or spiritual, or sacramental impulse behind much of the writing returned this work to its origins in the middle class and in romanticism.

This bit of literary history may not be of much use. To Gombrowicz no doubt it would amount to a kind of genealogical preening. For myself, I see that it is, like the rest of this lecture, in its subterranean way, a response to the Peruvian poet who spoke about the little personal poems of American poets. It's an effort to describe how the work of catching something of the reality of these most common and difficult human relationships in language came to be taken up by American poets and to say something about why it matters. If there were more room, it would be interesting to try to describe as well how in the past thirty years the burden of the tactic of identifying one's personal suffering with the diseases of the age has fallen away from the autobiographical enterprise and made some of the human and writerly issues, once they were free of what is potentially falsifying in that apocalyptic ambition, perhaps truer and more difficult. I'm not sure what Adrian Zelinski would make of Sylvia Plath's assertions that what the speaker in her poems suffered from her father was the equivalent of what the Jews of Europe suffered from the Germans. Most of the younger writers have in this followed the way of Williams rather than of Eliot and Pound. They have perhaps tried to understand history, but they are not in competition with its terrors.

Which brings me to the White Business in the Trees. It is a phrase in "Celestial Music," a poem in Louise Glück's new book *Ararat. Ararat* is a sequence of poems about a family, two sisters and a mother after the death of the father. It belongs decisively to the genre of family poems that are about fate, though it is also about children, about a third generation. The language of the poems is spare, remarkably devoid of explicit metaphors. The verse has Glück's characteristic severity and beauty, though I think it is supposed to be a little more relaxed and conversational than her usual idiom. And nothing happens in the book. It is a world becalmed, and not exactly by grief, as one poem explains:

> No one could write a novel about this family:
> too many similar characters. Besides, they're all women;
> there was only one hero.
>
> Now the hero's dead. Like echoes, the women last longer;
> they're all too tough for their own good.
>
> From this point on, nothing changes:
> there's no plot with a hero.
> In this house, when you say *plot* what you mean is love story.
> The women can't get moving.
> Oh, they get dressed, they eat, they keep up appearances.

The animation in the family, one gathers, had been provided by the competition among the women for the attention of the father, a rather distant figure, so that his removal not only absents the motive for action but lays bare its inner workings in a way that leaves the women languid. Thus the lack of incident. It is a sort of female version of Hamlet's dilemma in which the problem is that there was no murder and no return of the ghost. And the writing about this is somewhere between merciless and wry. But it would be to mis-hear the poems not to hear underneath their sometimes ruthless, sometimes funny, and always cool surface an intense sadness—that pathos that I have said interested me. Over and over the poems seem to say that to feel is to feel hurt, that the object of feeling is inadequate, that the true forms of the feeling are therefore the deflected ones, envy, resignation. This gets stated, in a way that is also characteristic of Glück, in a series of paradoxes, cruelly plain: "the face of love, to her, / is the face turning away", "the one who has nothing wins", "they are sisters, savages", "the best way / to love us was to not / spend time with us." The sadness comes because, for all the ferocity and toughness and unwillingness to be deceived in the writing, it never averts its face from this scene. There is no question, no real possibility of simply turning away. And the pathos is in that, in the depth of the attachment.

That's why I think the book begins with the speaker's sense of being wounded. It is the first thing we hear when we open the pages of the book:

> Long ago, I was wounded.
> I learned
> to exist, in reaction,
> out of touch
> with the world: I'll tell you
> what I meant to be—
> a device that listened.
> Not inert: still.
> A piece of wood. A stone.

This rhymes for me in remarkable ways with Allen Ginsberg's struggle in *Kaddish* between feeling and deadness, hope and an imprisoning sense of fate. This self-division is turned in the final line of the poem into a sort of debate between the transcendence of prayer and the cawing of crows:

> Lord Lord Lord caw caw caw

It is also apparent in Ginsberg's account of the composition of *Kaddish,* which, unpunctuated, unresigned, determined to be in touch, but ambiguous about the reality of the things we touch, seems to speak from the same experience:

> In the midst of the broken consciousness of mid twentieth century suffering anguish of separation from my own body and its natural infinity of feeling its own self one with all self I instinctively seeking to reconstitute that blissful union which I experienced so rarely I took it to be supernatural and gave it holy Name thus made hymn laments of longing and litanies of triumphancy of Self over the mind-illusion mechano-universe of unfeeling Time in which I saw my self my own mother and my very nation trapped desolate our worlds of consciousness homeless and at war except for the original trembling of bliss in breast and belly of every body that nakedness rejected in suits of fear that familiar defenceless living hurt

> self which is myself same as all others abandoned scared to our own unchanging desire for each other.

Odd that it could describe the work of both Ginsberg and Glück: "thus made hymn laments of longing and litanies of triumphancy of Self over the mind-illusion mechano-universe of unfeeling Time." But it does.

In this early stage of his work Ginsberg's visionary hopefulness has an optimistically blurred quality. You cannot tell for sure if he thinks the wound can be healed in Time, if Time can be made to feel. Later, as his religious practice deepens, one can see that he doesn't think so. His elsewhere, unlike Adrian Zelinski's, is cosmic. There never was this optimism in Glück and so her work was from the beginning tragic in tone, but pulled toward life in time by sorrow, by a sense of tenderness toward being. This is figured in *Ararat* in the poem called "Celestial Music." She is speaking of a friend who counsels her to love life on earth:

> In my dreams, my friend reproaches me. We're walking
> on the same road, except it's winter now;
> she's telling me that when you love the world you hear celestial music:
> look up, she says. When I look up, nothing.
> Only clouds, snow, a white business in the trees
> like brides leaping to a great height—
> Then I'm afraid for her; I see her
> caught in a net deliberately cast over the earth—

It is a startling moment in this book almost free of metaphor—the snow in the branches, which is always a little like blossoms, as a bride caught there. It is a sort of Kore myth transposed upward, a gnostic retelling in which the love of life, the moment of its blossoming and ceremony, traps us. I had spoken of the split subject in these narratives of family, the distance between the remembering adult artist and the vulnerable wishing child. Here, as in *Kaddish,* this separation feels like a tearing. The space between which art makes use of, which feeling fills, is attachment to life. This is what the last lines of *Ararat* say:

> in childhood, I thought
> that pain meant
> I was not loved.
> It meant I loved.

This is perhaps a place to end. But I wanted to say another word about the lines in "Celestial Music." What is moving about them is that we sense the language is the father's language. The phrase that summarizes both nature and desire so dismissively, the "white business in the trees," seems to come directly out of the particular idiom of a family, of a time and a place. It is another kind of net, that language, the one the world gives us to cast so that we might catch in it a little of what it is and what we are, and we are, among other things, the poverties of the language we inherit. Poignant to see it registered so scrupulously. *Ararat is* new to me. I'm not sure I've got hold of the whole book yet, particularly on the issues of fate and art and the generations, which it tries to confront so unblinkingly. In the past when I've thought about Adrian Zelinski yearning toward freedom, I've thought of *Kaddish* and Lowell's "Memories of West Street and Lepke" and Elizabeth Bishop's "In the Waiting Room," these American poems from the happy cities with their burdens of sorrow and fatality and grief, each of them an instance of the bravery of art. And if that seems like praise, discreet or not, of poetry, then it is a good place to end.

What We Write, Why We Write It, and Who Cares

Richard Ford

It's probably not a novelist's proper calling to give lectures. Philip Larkin called writers standing up in front of audiences, "me pretending to be me." But it's a chance we jump at because it's so much easier than writing stories. In lectures, glibness is acceptable, sometimes even appreciated—whereas in actual writing it usually isn't. At the lectern you get "help" from your actual voice and persona being already more or less in place, whereas in stories you have to start new every time. The many disparate opinions, biases, vindictivenesses that usually float around useless in your head can in a talk like this be corralled and advertised as: "a far-ranging, widely-referential, no-holds-barred address stressing the value of Mr. Ford's age and experience."

And finally, of course, in a lecture there's the promise which real writing doesn't offer: that if the content's no good, or not even there, it'll quickly be forgotten and do no harm as we float off toward cocktail hour.

On the other hand, writing and its more august cousin, literature, are permanent. Once we commit them, they last forever. And, in a sense, what I want to talk about commences and ends in that important fact.

I've been away from the university for what seems like a long time—twelve years—and away from this one for nearly sixteen. But when I was here, writing a novel for the first time, and being a stuffed-shirt Junior Fellow in the Society of Fellows, teaching creative writing, and being a cringing preceptor for Mr. Weisbuch's introductory literature course, I frankly thought it was just great here. This was before the deconstructionists took a stranglehold on the Modern Language Association, and started turning students of literature against literature. Then,

---

The Hopwood Lecture, 1992

at least, beginning in 1971, it seemed to me that literary study, and literature itself, and "writing" were all part of one continuum, and that I was in the world here—the applause of my colleagues was the world's applause; their disapproval or indifference a credible cultural milieu for the writing I was beginning to do. I have no wish to overturn that view now. I was encouraged and welcomed here and my status as a nonentity wasn't held against me. I was here to learn, not just to perform.

It's true that in the years between then and now my experience of the university in general has made me think that literary study, imaginative literature itself, and ongoing writing, are more of a continuum-by-consent than a manifestation of some natural law. And beyond that, I've been struck by how much of university life is involved with the practice of judging—judging others, their acts, their attitudes, making discriminations, assigning moral values, and conversely, by how much of life outside the university is not concerned with that, indeed hardly has time for it.

My first evidence of this judging came, in fact, in 1975, when my office-mate over in Haven Hall (we'll call him Professor Jones) explained to me one afternoon—one in which in his absence I'd dispensed some good-willed but he thought incorrect "instruction" to some of his students about how to pronounce some Middle English vowels in *The Canterbury Tales,* that (he explained) *Writers really didn't belong in the university, that it was not the correct place for us. We could be here for a while, okay. But we needed, he felt, to be out living our lives, having adventures, finding things to write about.* I don't remember if he finally said where our place actually was. Just elsewhere. Out. This—the university—was his place. He did seem certain of that.

But in truth, I had no body of specialized knowledge to teach. I had no controversial research underway requiring the university's shelter. In fact I had no real care about aiding young women and men to become writers—especially not at the expense of my own desires, which were to write novels. It may just've been as Eudora Welty wrote about herself, that I "lacked the instructing turn of mind." And so, shortly after this conversation and for reasons related to it, I departed the university. It was, as the saying goes, one of my "earliest influences," one of the negative ones I had to try to turn into profit.

So, I know acutely—and poignantly on a day like today—that now is an influential time in the life of you young writers. The barely conscious convictions you begin to form now about who reads, and how well, and where's the ideal destination for your work, what are the right elevations to set for your seriousness of purpose, and what should you be writing about, and what public tolerance for your work can you rely on—where's your "place" in other words—these'll have to direct and console you for your whole life.

Thinking about these same things, myself, I sense in the American air now an unhappy censoriousness—something much different from when I began writing stories in the sixties, even though I thought I began at a time of relative aesthetic and political tumult. But from all angles I hear people saying "no" to someone else. We can hear it in our politics and political processes: people telling us what we can't do. Few people seem willing to admit or say "yes" to much of anything; and both as a cause and as an effect, there's a wide feeling of bad apprehension and distaste for current life, a national feeling actually of powerlessness even to perceive accurately our private lives; a hunger for governance; a lack of courage. In many parts of America the powers that be would rather you own and use a Mac-10 than *The Catcher in the Rye.*

Obviously, this censoriousness is perceptible in the arts; and not just in the high administrative levels which control, for instance, the NEA and the NEH, but a censoriousness among ground-level commentators—often novelists themselves—saying "no" to this, "no" to that, unable it seems to like something without disliking something else—a habit more typical of critics than artists.

* Tom Wolfe complains in *Harper's* magazine that there are actually good subjects and bad ones, and practically all contemporary novels but the one he wrote are neurasthenic because they don't choose—or at least he doesn't perceive them to have chosen—to reflect recent social history or economics or immigration patterns—the way he thinks Balzac did, or Trollope.

* Edward Hoagland, the distinguished essayist, complains in *Esquire* that very little's good at all in current American literature.

* Patricia Hampl complains inexplicably in the *New York Times* that there's something second-rate about writing in the first person.

* Madison Bell complains that minimalism (whatever that is) has eroded the longueurs within the American narrative impulse—the antidote being to write like Peter Taylor, or by implication, like Mr. Bell, himself.

It is, I hardly need to say, a Republican mood—pinched and conservative, peremptory and uncharitable, dismissive and afraid, a national temper in which it's appealing to shout art down. Though simultaneously, of course, in such an unpretty national temper, the arts take on a very special and resuscitative responsibility (a bad time in the world is often a good time for art). Indeed, in these moments of powerlessness the impulse to write or read a novel ought to be a saving impulse.

Consequently, I've thought to myself from time to time lately that it might be hard starting out writing today—during a period in universities when stories and novels were reduced to being texts said to mean the opposite of what they evidently mean and what their privileged authors rashly thought they meant; when literature was treated as bankrupt and boring, and a writer a figure of fun for writing it; and when what you thought was no good was actually deemed excellent—only you weren't the right race or the right sexual orientation or the right gender to understand what excellence is.

I know I'm sensitive to this peculiar air we all breathe and that's supposed to inspire us: I write novels myself, and this mood influences my work and how I think about literature, just as I'm sure whether you know it or not it influences you—influences what you choose to write about, what you will and won't take credit for, what you believe literature is and what it isn't. It's certain that some of what feels like moral imperative now will pass, and seem like a vogue in five years. So, it's important for us all to decide—by looking closely at the world and at language—what's worth accepting and what's not.

I have a friend who teaches at a major Eastern university near Boston. He's a writer like I am, and he teaches creative writing. And last autumn, a young male student turned in for class a particularly graphic story in which a good deal of heterosexual fornication was described in vivid documentary detail culminating in an act of climactic anal intercourse. The story was read and given if not exactly loving at least respectful treatment by the class, except for a young woman who said that such writing as this was not literature, and shouldn't even be allowed into the dignity of class discussion. Women were being degraded in this story, she felt. She thereafter went home and wrote and turned in for class an even more vivid and detailed story of heterosexual roguery *also* eventuating in a climactic anal intercourse—which I guess is now the *ne plus ultra* in heterosexuality—whereupon the class and my novelist friend deemed this her best work.

But the young woman was stricken. She felt she'd written her story as a protest, to outrage and anger her colleagues and to illustrate for them their errors by putting them into the distressing place she'd occupied before: certainly a time-honored use for literature. She felt she'd carefully calculated the response of her audience, yet unfortunately she'd been wrong—which is, of course, one, though only one measure of writing's success or excellence.

My friend told me this story a bit in the Art Linkletter spirit of "kids saying the darndest things." We were both of us amused. But we were surprised by the events as a small but serious piece of ethical business. The young woman in question (and it might as easily have been a young man) had failed to appreciate not only that her claim to write such a story in protest was equal to the previous young man's claim to write his to titillate or annoy. She likewise seemed not to appreciate what, in fact, was the inspiration for her own story (Larkin wrote once that "One of the reasons one writes is that all existing books are somehow unsatisfactory"). And beyond that, and even more worrisome to me, was her choice not only to exercise her freedom to write what she pleased when it suited her, but also to violate her own apparent criteria for good literature when she felt she had a high enough purpose for doing so. I couldn't help feeling at the time the similarity on a small scale to the situation Bret Ellis faced in publishing *American Psycho* two years ago—that being a book, curiously enough, more people wished to condemn and suppress than read, but which quickly disappeared not because it was suppressed but because the culture dealt with it ultimately and proportionately as a book—not as a war-crime.

This past September, I took a trip to Sweden, to take part in a colloquium on multiculturalism at the University of Lund. Lund, I was told at the time, was Sweden's Yale. Whereas Uppsala was its Harvard. I never found out where its Michigan was. And, this is what writers do now instead of going to war, something also easier than writing—colloquializing in foreign countries. Spreading American influence.

Present in Lund were a "Native American Female Poet"; a "Native American Male Professor" from the University of San Diego; a Fulbright Professor of American Studies representing the U.S. State Department—and me. And while we were addressing as a panel a group of Swedish journalists and students of American culture, giving witness to the convergent and variegated forces of ethnicity and race and gender in our society, I happened to observe that I was the token Living White Male in our group. And when I said this, I noticed a ripple of discomfort go across my colleagues' faces. And in the course of continuing our panel I was asked eventually by the moderator if I myself had a Native American heritage. And, natch, I did. And thereafter on several occasions I was told that I was not really a Token Living White Male, but in fact was arguably a Native American, myself—that is, their kind of Native American, not the kind I already thought I was.

This of course was amusing to me since not so long ago, practically everybody I knew was claiming to be part Cherokee as a way of one-upping somebody else. It became a cultural cliché, after which there dawned a period of rather severe credential checking and loudly expressed indignity over the Indian's sole ability to speak for the Indian.

In my own family, our Indian-ness was always a subject of some dystrophic unease. My great-grandmother had been born on the Osage Strip in Oklahoma and had married a non-Indian and moved across the border into Arkansas, where apparently there weren't as many Indians. Thereafter there was a considerable scramble in my grandmother's generation to keep their Indian-ness quiet and to seem like what they thought were regular white people—Irish and Germans. This issue eventually devolved upon my mother as ethnicity often does upon succeeding generations: clumsily. From time to time she gave evidence of believing Indians were second-class humans, but then she would fight you if you said so. There was a good deal of looking at our profiles and wondering if they "seemed Indian," and making wry insider jokes about "Italian Indians" in the movies, and admiring the Navajos for baffling the Japanese cryptographers in World War II, and shaking our heads about what a raw deal Jim Thorpe got from the Olympic Committee. There even began to be some lack of clarity about whether we were actually Osage or Cherokee, ourselves—if indeed we were Indians at all.

But here now in Sweden I was being unexpectedly conscripted into the tribe, so to speak, and for reasons I had to think about, since I hadn't wanted to be. And the reason I felt I was being made an ad hoc member—I came to believe this later—was not so much so I'd feel at one with anybody, but so that I'd feel I spoke for others and not just for myself, or for whomever I might've thought I spoke for; and, importantly, so that I would try to calculate or modulate what I said in behalf of not offending the putative beliefs of unnamed others.

I'd been made part not just of a tribe, but of a special interest group, which depending on the Indian or the professor you spoke to, had a way of looking at things, and perhaps a way of looking askance at or of casting aspersions on non-members. Something about me—my good will or my complex sense of myself, or my freedom from some cultural biases and clichés, or indeed my own experience with my own past, or maybe just my willingness to see myself as I chose to, wasn't exactly being credited.

And I didn't like that, no more than I like hearing somebody say what should or shouldn't be read. Not that I wanted to speak for all Living White Males any more than I wanted to speak for Native Americans—whom I wasn't very familiar with as a group. I was in fact just making a little multicultural joke—jokes being a rare commodity in multicultural circles.

As a writer, I don't believe in "groups." Generalities—about women or men, or blacks or whites—have never been sufficiently consistent with my experience. A kind of truth-telling god lives only in details for me. That's one of literature's appealing conceits—that it is specific and often takes as one of its challenges to test with details (even invented details) the truth of conventional wisdom, and even to supplant that putative wisdom if it's found lacking. What I wanted was to speak not *for* my group but simply *from* myself—even if I might've been wrong, offensive, or finally chastised. Indeed, I wanted to imagine not what made me or Native people special; but what made me—a non-native—like them. What made us alike.

To me this is what multiculturalism is worth—in colloquiums and in writing short stories and novels; it's an invitation to imagine more meticulously the distinctions and similarities which make us able to share the planet together; it's an opportunity to challenge and if need be break the hold of conventional wisdom, of history, and to complicate our responses on behalf of extending the benefice of sympathy to others who aren't just like us but may be more like us than we know. Good intentions, of course, don't make good literature. There's still the obligation in exercising free sway about humanity to get it right. But I'd rather risk doing my best and getting it wrong and being ignored and castigated than to be scared off by what a University of Chicago sociologist recently referred to as the "hegemonic vision of single-minded interest groups," which—to me—is nothing but a lower form of ward-heeling, small-time power politics where truth is not the goal.

To my mind, one good definition of a political issue is an important human issue somebody decides to treat politically, just as a political novel is a piece of persuasive art somebody decides to treat as politics.

There's a sentiment which says you can't just speak *from* yourself, that you can only represent your group, and all is politics. Be that as it may be, those determinations are usually made after the fact of artistic utterance, in an attempt to influence the future. And I merely try not to be misled about my own first principle: that I'm responsible for my book, and nobody else is.

During the writing of five books and a relatively short time as a writer—sixteen years since the first novel I wrote was published—I've had my share of influential forces worked on me. And in that time I've tried to be faithful and stay alert to what I was ignorant of so I could see my miscues and not go on making them. But, I've been accused of being a racist in the *New Yorker* because a reviewer thought a character in *The Sportswriter* had insensitive racial views. I've been accused off and on of having "problems with women," though my accusers were almost always men. I've been accused of being cruel to animals any number of times, and of condescending to the "lower classes," although I don't believe in class distinctions. I've been accused of writing "male books," of being a phony westerner, a failed southerner, and to having no right even to write about the people I've written about. I've been told in print, in the *Washington Post,* that I actually had no subject at all and should quit writing; and that a rather simple-seeming book of mine which I thought was just about a young Montana boy growing up in the world, being abandoned at home with his mother and once inadvertently seeing her naked one night, was actually a book about incest—an accusation which I didn't think was true but which frankly troubled me.

I've had it the other way, too: some good reviews that said I was doing a good job—though I don't mean to confuse book reviews with serious judgment. My friend Joyce Carol Oates has told me on several occasions that I wrote very strong and good and convincing female characters. I often find myself clinging to that endorsement like a piece of thin driftwood. And if it's true I attribute it to giving my female characters as many good dialogue lines—lines that possess drama or the potential for affecting human action—as I give to my male characters.

Once, indeed, I wrote a story in which a little Anglo-Canadian girl tells a young Blackfeet boy that "An Indian is just another bump in the road to me." And shortly after that I got a phone call from a professor at the University of North Carolina wanting to know what I knew about "young Indian men lying out on public highways at night," since his research showed this was a frequent cause of death among male native

Americans. I had to tell him that I hadn't done any research on the subject. I'd just hit upon that line one morning, liked it and left it in the story trusting that if I could think of it, somebody'd certainly already done it. In other words, I'd just made it up without knowing so much about Indians, but having spent my life paying attention to human beings. Such, I guess, is the uncanny power of the imagination if not reliably to find truth—at least to shed light on new facts, which if we're persuaded by them become truth.

To bring this set of concerns down to a less politically-sensitive level, I think of writing about humans somewhat as I think of writing about places. In Kim Townsend's biography of Sherwood Anderson he claims that Anderson wrote so well about northern Ohio because he hadn't lived there in a long time and had forgotten all about it. Anderson invented Ohio using bits of memory, and using a habit and affection for language with which to give literary body to the strong, unarticulated feelings and torques he was subject to. And it's somewhat in this way that many writers make characters, recognizing as Paul West wrote about Robbe-Grillet, that language is a "uniquely human and subjective thing to begin with, and it can never with utter authority reveal the nature of anything," people and places included, though language can certainly invent what we then believe.

The impulse to choose a line of dialogue which eventually will be understood as a component of a character is in some ways similar to the impulse to choose, for example, to set your story in a place called Winesburg, or in Great Falls. Admittedly, in the case of Great Falls, there's a town out there on the plains of Montana. But the Great Falls in *my* stories bears more resemblance to Anderson's Winesburg than to some actual place: it's made up principally of its name—Great Falls, a two-word combination I like (the long A sound giving way to the short A; an appealing iambic or, if you choose, trochaic foot; the idiosyncratic picture it puts in my head; the appearance of its letters on the page—these among other qualities I ascribe to it).

These spontaneous, sensory, rather less-cognitive considerations are close to how I chose the line I had my little Canadian girl say to her Indian friend and that then became part of her character and his, and turned out to be the object of someone's "distinguished research": I just liked the line. I thought it was vivid, raw, memorable, funny.

I chose Great Falls, in fact, before I'd ever been to the actual place or knew much about it. I just sensed for some of the reasons I've just said, that it was for me what the poet Richard Hugo called a "Triggering Town"—a name, a place that provoked me to write sentences and from whose earthly actuality I needed to be free so I could write something new.

Later on, of course, I'm free to return to my sentences, as we do. I can decide if I want to use Great Falls, if it makes sense, if I'm using it in an interesting way; or, in the other case, if I want to be the author of a line that says, "An Indian is just a bump in the road to me"; does it mean, if I write it, I have to believe that sentiment myself? Can this woman's character survive it? Can the story go on to something redeeming? Okay, maybe I'm compensating, in my unconscious, for an ambiguous feeling about my family's disputed Native American heritage, and I'm trying in writing a line like that to obliterate it. Freudian or multicultural critics can declare about that, if the story's any good, once they've read it.

But I wish primarily to be close to that which seems like early impulse—as romantic as it might be—the one that brings words and phrases to my consideration early. It's the impulse Miss Welty described as a writer "writing at his own emergency." I know that when I fret that I've lost it, the "it" is always that—the impulse to associate freely and haphazardly in language and in the ideas and associations words carry with them, to play loose with the ordinary ways of organizing the world in words.

Stephen Spender once wrote in his journal that Louis McNeice knew everything he thought and had a clear response to everything he experienced. But I'm not like that; and I doubt, frankly, if McNeice was either. Things come into my rather chaotic mind—bits of language, self-awareness—and they hide there, swirling and randomly attaching and separating like electrons, coming back, if ever, into consciousness or onto the page sometimes profoundly reconstituted. And it is indeed there, in that inchoate stage of writing-which-is-actually-thinking, that I suspect great invention and surprise and new intelligence occur. In a writing life in which you try to keep yourself open to random experience, it's unwanted and also impossible to keep yourself entirely "uninfluenced" at this early stage. But it's at least worthwhile to think where the surprises in your work come from.

I believe—and you probably do, too, at least in principle—that it's sometimes literature's project to outrage and offend and to shock and upbraid and make readers uncomfortable, and that Randall Jarrell was right when he said that we need to be sure our writing offends the right people. (In reviewing Richard Wilbur's poems in 1951, he wrote rather self-interestedly that, "If you never look just wrong to your contemporaries you will never look just right to posterity—every writer has to be to some extent, sometimes, a law unto himself.")

Though putting up personally with being a law unto oneself is an ambiguous and often unpleasant and ethically precarious business for a writer. On the one hand, of course, we're aided by our ignorance, and by slogans about our putative freedoms. We're too young, many of us, to remember those famous books which were a law unto themselves and were actually banned—*Ulysses, Lady Chatterly's Lover,* more recently *Huckleberry Finn* and *Catch 22*. And then my friend Rushdie; well, we may think, he's sort of an Englishman and far away, and maybe we didn't think *The Satanic Verses* was worth it anyway. He certainly outraged the wrong people, and has been subject to considerable influences upon his freedoms. But maybe we think he should've been more prudent.

Myself, in truth, I don't like outraging people, and I don't mean my work to offend, and actually think that it shouldn't. I worry when people say to me I should quit writing, or that I write "male" books. (Though there are other days when I worry that my books are tame, not offensive enough, and that I'm not a technical innovator). In any case, I don't want to be unduly affected by reactions to my books such that I might next time decide differently what to write or not to write. If I continue, I want to feel free to write whatever I think I can write well. I want my stories, if they can, to affect readers in the way great literature has affected me: to be the ax for the frozen sea within us; to be, as Dürrenmatt wrote, a rebel against death.

It is one of the privileges of being a writer, and likewise one of its high prices, that we intend the effect of what we write to be permanent, and accept responsibility for it. Proportionate to our aspirations, we can't escape responsibility, for example, for those effects of our writing that naturally and reasonably come into the purview of "multiculturalism," or "race consciousness," or "sexual orientation," or gender concerns—because, most intimately, those are human concerns. And in any case, the world out there, the world that has no interest in anything as privileged as imaginative writing, has now ordained these concerns as facts.

Free as we are, writers do come to these issues—as least in our work—differently from other people. Freedom and Art are not institutions, and as writers—just as is true of filmmakers or photographers or painters—no one has a claim on us. We employ no one, we give no one tenure, we have no clients, or fiduciary relationships; we're not *in loco parentis,* and we owe no one fairness unless we choose to. Writers are not required to be democratic. And our obligation is not to flatter you, or to create positive role models, but to try at the height of our aspiration to tell you something you didn't know about a subject you care for, and which once you know it, becomes essential. We expect a voluntary audience if we have one at all. And consequent to such freedoms as these, we accept—even if we don't exactly relish—marginality in our culture.

From time to time, in variable moods, I've wondered how I can make my stories be *more* "multicultural," more sensitive. Whom I can stop oppressing, whom I can appreciate more in my own workplace? Should I have more narrators be women, or maybe Mexican women (though perhaps I can't because I'm not a Mexican woman myself). Maybe I should have more white males be hoodwinked by clever lesbians who are CEOs of large corporations, or more gay men be brain surgeons, or more African Americans be Supreme Court Justices.

In actual practice, it might suit me to write about a minority character in an unflattering light, some light which doesn't corroborate all of humanity's best possibilities. I might have a woman get socked in the mouth, or portrayed as a prostitute. I might decide to have a living white male depicted as a figure of fun or even killed. I may diminish one character, flatten another, if I think the whole justifies it, if I can say to myself that I take this decision proportionate to a high aim, to discovering something important—such as the connection, as James wrote, between "bliss and bale." Or if I can answer affirmatively the question: does my writing it this way make any good difference in the world?

And maybe someone will think any one of these decisions makes my book no good. And if he does think that, what he can do is not read it. But unless *I* choose it, he can't stop me.

In the news a month ago you might remember there was a story about the film *Basic Instinct,* an especially fatuous and egregious bit of movie prurience. Gay and lesbian groups didn't like this movie, and protested it publicly, threatened to shut down theatres; there had been efforts to obstruct the actual making of this film by cutting electrical lines and disrupting the movie's production. These groups were offended that lesbians and bisexuals, all of whom I guess they represented, were in the movie depicted as homicidal—which the lesbians and bisexuals actually portrayed in the movie certainly were.

And this strikes me several ways at once. First, I think it's the right of interested people to protest what they don't like and to make their feelings and thoughts known. I think it's at the very least defensible that they argue for a benigner public perception—for sympathy. But I think it is not their right nor is it right forcibly to suppress the making of this movie or any movie inasmuch as doing so takes their own freedom and sets it against itself in a stupefying way.

Living in and around Mississippi, as I do, I think about Miss Welty a lot these days. In a letter to her literary agent in 1942 she commented upon what she called rival validities, by which she meant *actuality* as it's encountered upon the page (in her case, short stories) and *actuality* as it's encountered outside of books—actuality in the world so to speak. She was being urged at the time by editors, powerful people in New York who, like movie producers, thought they were mindful of what were the tastes of the American readership—an urge which almost always establishes a low water mark. They wanted her to write stories that seemed to them "more like life."

Only that wasn't what she cared to do, even at the cost of being kept out of print. Her belief of course was that her stories—stories that offended no one, I suspect—were good the way they were, and that what was on the page had its own sovereign validity. And what underlies her claim is the conviction that what comes to the page is free—free to be what it is, free from any allegiance to how somebody other than the writer thinks the world or literature is, or should be, or shouldn't.

Art always thrives as some function of freedom, which isn't to say that oppression will kill it, only impede it, and deprive some of us of its generosity and its light. To accord others freedom is, however, not such a noteworthy virtue when you *agree* with what they're doing. It's only a great virtue when you agree to allow what you don't like. It is that odd, uneasy, vertiginous quality of art—that it may surprise you and tell you things you won't like to know—which makes it different from politics. And it is also this quality of art which makes it so fragile and precious and attractive.

When people suppress art—a movie, a book, a collection of photographs showing a representation of Christ in a tray filled with urine—the target of that suppression is usually, at least in this contemporary and moralizing atmosphere, thought to be the artist, who's stopped from making what he wishes to make because his rights are said to interfere with the passive unspecified rights of others. But the actual and more vulnerable victim of such suppression is the audience who's stopped by others from seeing something which might affect them, stopped from reading what might illuminate the world for them by shocking them, by turning the world or language in a way it never was seen to be and thereby revealing the world clearly. Indeed, suppressing art stops us even from being able to exercise a valuable moral or aesthetic judgment by saying, "no, I don't like that. I see that, and I reject that sensibility. I seek the beautiful and that's not it."

Real censorship—and that's ultimately what we're talking about—is not merely a personal attack which says, "you can't say that," but one which insidiously says, "you can't hear that; you can't think that; you can't know that." It's an impulse which caters to moral lassitude in all of us.

As Rushdie wrote long before he became a victim of oppression and censorship, and I quote him from his book *Imaginary Homelands,* "Literature is not in the business of copywriting certain themes for certain groups. . . [indeed]. . . the most insidious effect of censorship is that, in the end, it can deaden the imagination of people. Where there is no debate, it is hard to go on remembering, every day, that there is a suppressed side to every argument. It becomes almost impossible to conceive of what the suppressed things might be. It becomes easy to think that what has been suppressed was valueless, anyway, or so dangerous that it needed to be suppressed."

Confoundingly enough, it may even be in universities that subtle forms of oppression find a home. Universities, after all, are places where a rather inert politeness unknown elsewhere in the world dominates, so that varying ideas (good and bad—and there *are* bad ideas) are often viewed as having the same neutralizing weight; where scholars write without the expectation of a large readership so that the possible crucialness of any single piece of new writing is less felt. Writing programs themselves (and I went to one) stress the importance of writing and the romantic sovereignty of the writer herself or himself, more than they stress the destination of writing and its most important power—readers and their need to be told things.

The basic character of the academy is conserving and self-preservation, whereas the nature of art is to be on the "dangerous edge of things." Art is frail, and optional and precarious (we hardly need to be protected from it). But the academy is armored against frailty by a history of great books and great thought and great writing already done. It may be, simply, that here truth may seem more available than it really is, less a matter requiring personal courage and vision.

My former teacher, Mr. Doctorow, who, I know, once delivered the Hopwood Lecture, spoke last October to a committee of the Congress in defense of the National Endowment for the Arts, and he remarked then on what he called "the latent underlying jealousy we have for elevated expression that is personal, uninvited and powerful, that almost automatic anger we have for a kind of witness and truth-telling that is not endorsed or accredited by church, or corporation or family, or other governing institution of our society."

Jealousy or conservatism or whatever are the other forms of timidness which lead to censorship do indeed press peculiarly upon the contemporary arts by assuming their existence matters somehow less than the apparently unsuppressed art of times past—whose excellence we come to take for granted, though they may only be survivors of some other kind of oppressive society.

But that sort of bias, for a writer, propounds a lie, because there's no reason to suppose that work going on this afternoon is likely to be less excellent than work which came into being a hundred years ago. In fact, there may be good reasons to expect quite the opposite.

The larger point here, having said these few words about artistic freedom, is not so much to boast that "I can write what I want and no one can stop me," but rather it's a point less certain of answer but much to the heart of what it is to be a good writer—a fact young writers have to address somehow and so do I, and not just once but again and again. That old white, middle-class literary critic, Lionel Trilling, wrote it this way, in 1940: "A culture is not a flow, nor even a confluence: the form of its existence is struggle—or at least debate—[and] it is nothing if not a dialectic." The challenge for any writer of high aspiration is this: given my quarrel with a culture complexer than I ever guessed, how with my freedom intact can I be better? It's art's premise, after all, that there can be better. And it's not enough merely to do what you're free to do. The challenge is to change, adapt, find new means, new enthusiasms, to move past the limitations of vogue and politics and most cunningly past your own fear that you can't do it.

Richard Shweder, the University of Chicago sociologist I mentioned a while ago, wrote on the Op-Ed Page in the *New York Times* that " . . . the authority of a voice ought to reside in what it says and not in who says it . . . [T]o grow is to exceed the limits of parochial experience . . , [and] people have written brilliantly about cultures and genders other than their own . . . our humanity [being after all] polymorphous and complex."

And so, to be better, I take that as my own premise: to exceed the limits of parochial experience in what I write; and to try, using my little freedoms, even occasionally moderating them, to represent mankind not so as to endear myself but so as to dignify it by insisting on its humanity and its complexity, its finality.

And I try harder. I try to stay thoughtful of what is humanity's best self. If I diminish a character, make assaults on humankind in some way, I try eventually to replenish the account in other ways; and I don't part with a book unless I feel I've authorized every line.

The feminist literary critic, Carolyn Heilbrun, wrote more than a decade ago that "Today's youth, whatever the reasons, no longer go to literature and what we used to call 'culture' as to the fountain of wisdom and experience. Youth . . . responds rather to an alternative culture, outside the English classroom, vital, challenging, relevant, and usually electronically transmitted. . . . If students are to see literature as capable of informing them about any of the aspects of life, they must become convinced that literature is as capable of revolutionary exploration as their own lives are."

Ms. Heilbrun made this observation in behalf of teaching feminist criticism, a good cause. I borrow it now in behalf of saying to you writers who're very likely writing the books the next generation will be reading in universities and that critics will be explaining, that you must re-vision in some humane spirit the orthodoxies that seem even new to you now. (Since mostly they're already just the conventional wisdoms posing as taboos.) And do it as a way of attracting readers to literature. Or else you'll leave to the David Dukes and Pat Buchanans and Jean-Marie Le Pens of the world to decide what art is and who ought to get to see it.

My modest hope for young writers—those of you who won these awards and those who didn't and who might just as easily become good writers—is the same hope I have for myself and for readers: that you not be timid. That you not let others make you that way; that you not think that being a writer is just another profession with another set of networks to master, another ladder to climb, another set of well-placed elders to impress. Since there's no one who can tell you what to write, or how to do it, you're entitled to your own vision, but it ought to be worth your life to put it to words the best you possibly can.

Nine Antirules of Journalism

Roger Rosenblatt

I dedicate half of this talk (I've never dedicated half of a talk before, or a whole talk if to comes to that) to Avery Hopwood who, among other things, became rich at writing plays, which seems to me noteworthy. They say about playwriting that you can't make a living at it, but you *can* make a killing.

I would like to dedicate the other half to Larry Goldstein, editor of the *Michigan Quarterly Review,* because of the anxiety I have caused him, and continue to cause him. He requested, quite reasonably, that I give him the printed copy of this talk. I informed him, quite unreasonably, that I don't write out my talks, but that if someone would care to record and transcribe it, that would be fine with me. Goldstein shuddered, and is shuddering still.

The reason I don't like to write out talks is that I don't like to read things aloud in public, and I kind of like the fear of not knowing exactly what I'll say. I kind of like to look at the fear in *your* eyes, too. I don't even like the title of this talk, but being magnanimous, I conceded to Goldstein a title: "Nine Antirules of Journalism." Then I realized that I had to come up with nine.

I am leery of titles from my experience of working at *Time* magazine. My colleagues and I used to collect the titles of books that we most favored. These are titles of real books that came in over the years. We had a special shelf on which we would keep them. Office favorites included *God and Vitamins, Socialism for the Dead,* an animal book called *Do Reindeer Experience Religious Ecstasy?* This was one of a whole series of animal books, which we discovered sell very well. Alan Coren, the former editor of *Punch,* was always trying to write a best seller. One day he asked his agent, "Well, what kind of books sell? I mean, on what subjects should I write books?" And his agent told him, Nazis, cats, or golf. So Coren wrote a book called *Golfing for Cats,* with a swastika on the

---

The Hopwood Lecture, 1993

cover. My own favorite title on our shelf was a book called *1637, a Year of No Significance*. And the absolute favorite of the boys in the office, a computer book called *Using Your Wang for Business*.

When I saw the distinguished roster of Hopwood lecturers before me, I realized that I also had no *authority* to give this talk. This was not news to me. I have no authority, generally. Every time I try to establish authority, I always bring humiliation upon myself.

When at *Time* I worked for a wonderful editor, Ray Cave—very dour man, had a beard, looked like Rockwell Kent's illustration of Captain Ahab. My family and I were living in Vermont when Cave called me, and I very much wanted to work at *Time*. But I didn't want to look over-eager. I didn't want to look like a hick. So I drove down to New York and had a conversation with Cave, in which everything sounded fine. The hours were fine. The salary was fine—in those days any salary would have been fine. Fifty dollars okay? Fine, fine. But I wanted to show Cave that I had some gumption. So I said, "Well" . . . my voice cracking because I was about to tell a lie. I said, "Well, I'm used to four weeks vacation." Now this was both true and not true. At the *Washington Post* where I had worked before, I got three weeks vacation, but at a university where I had worked before that, I got three *months* vacation. So I figured the whole thing averaged out. "Well," I said, "I'm used to four weeks vacation."

I looked at Cave. Cave looked at me. I could tell he could tell he wasn't dealing with any corn-fed. I could tell he could sense my authority.

"All right, Roger," he said after a pause. "We ordinarily start with five weeks, but in your case we'll make an exception."

I only had one experience in my life in which I managed to turn a humiliation into triumph. I've never told this story before. And the only reason I am recounting it at this university is that the incident involved a member of the English literature faculty here.

Richard Tillinghast and I were good friends at Harvard when we were in graduate school, and it so happened that we had our oral exam for our Ph.D. on the very same hour of the very same day. In graduate school I was quite undistinguished, quite unmemorable, but Richard was a star. Everybody knew Richard. That morning of our orals Richard and I decided to walk over to Warren House, where the English department was located, together. When we got to Warren House three professors greeted us, two congratulating me for being such a supportive friend as to walk Richard to his orals. One of the professors congratulating me happened to be on my board.

The orals began, Richard's taking place in the next room. I could clearly hear Richard's orals through the wall, as two of my examiners immediately went to sleep. I noticed that because the third examiner didn't show up. Meanwhile, through the wall I continued to hear raucous laughter, explosions of celebration. "That's great, Richard! Who would have thought of *that* before, Richard! Oh, the hell with this, Richard, let's go out and have a drink!" . . . while the tedium of my exam went on, and the seasons passed.

I interrupt this anecdote to bring you to another moment which I will then relate to the anecdote itself. Earlier in the year I was teaching a survey course in English literature. I like memorizing poetry, and I memorized Wordsworth's "Lines Composed a Few Miles Above Tintern Abbey," for two reasons. To show off was the first reason; and the second that it was easier to teach if I could just recite the poem freely and then talk about the lines. The students couldn't have cared less whether I had memorized the poem or not. Nonetheless, it rested in my mind throughout the term as I studied for my orals.

Back at the orals, where the professors are drowsily starting to awaken, the third examiner, an assistant professor, has finally remembered that this exam was to take place, and he bursts in the room wearing tennis togs, just off the court. He didn't want to appear foolish in front of his colleagues (he certainly didn't care how he looked before me), but he wanted to look like he was with it, you know, to rush into this exciting event with a question at the ready. "Where are we?" he asked the two others who, of course, could not answer that question.

One of them said, "Wordsworth."

"Wordsworth! Ah, Wordsworth!" said the assistant professor, as if he had just come from Wordsworth's cottage and a chat with Dorothy. "Wordsworth, Wordsworth, Wordsworth," he said. "Mr. Rosenthal . . ." he began. (Who were the other two to correct him? I didn't have the energy.) "Could you, Mr. Rosenthal, tell us how the poem, 'Lines Composed a Few Miles Above Tintern Abbey' begins?" Before that son-of-a-bitch settled his fat ass in that chair, I gave him the whole poem right between the eyes.

In his characteristically gracious introduction of me, Nick Delbanco referred to my most recent humiliation: my publisher suggesting that they publish a collection of my work. I know that this may sound lofty;

really it means that you're all washed up and that they just want to get the detritus out of the way and print the eight copies they send to reviewers, and then pension you off to some asylum. The humiliation consists of reading all the stuff that you've written, and realizing how little you are not suicidally ashamed of.

But I did discover something in the course of this investigation which became the seed of what I will try to make sense of today. I discovered that the one characteristic that defined this odd body of my work was mystery—not just the love of, or appreciation of, mystery, but a professional desire to dwell in mystery. I saw that it had done me good. That is, when I least understood a subject, when I was most overwhelmed with some experience, I was, strangely, most self-assured as a writer, most accurate as an observer.

It is in the interest of that idea of mystery that I concoct these nine antirules of journalism. These may be of use to those of you who would be journalists, but they really are intended to apply more generally to us as readers, writers, citizens, dealers in the experience of words. So I hope you won't mind if I present these antirules as if I were talking to young people about to enter that trade, because by this method I can most clearly state what I mean.

Let me start off simply by stating what these antirules are—you'll see why they are weird—and then I will try to explain them as I go along. 1) Be out of things, (2) Be slow, (3) Write dead stories, (4) Go to hell, (5) Distrust rational thought, (6) Be beside the point, (7) Avoid the company of people, (8) Betray your sources, and (9) the most important antirule, Do not understand it.

Be out of things. Oscar Levant said to Joan Crawford in *Humoresque,* "Don't blame me, lady, I didn't make the world; I barely live on it." That's the ticket. To be out of things you must create an atmosphere in which you deliberately generalize your knowledge and your experience. You must cultivate, believe it or not, the old general education. And this cultivation involves several decisions.

First, it involves the deliberate avoidance of the narrow focus, usually the assigned focus. If I could show all that journalism can and cannot do by using one movie, it would be *Citizen Kane,* which is largely about journalism. *Citizen Kane* is a wonderful example of how *not* to go about discovering a story.

You remember how *Citizen Kane* begins: there is the newsreel about all the high points of Charles Foster Kane's life spilling loudly on the screen, and then the newsreel winds down to that kind of awkward halt. The room is dark. The editor, unseen (always the best condition for an editor), says in effect to the reporters in the room, "Um, how do we go about this? I understand his last word was 'Rosebud.' Let's find out what Rosebud is. If we find out what Rosebud means, we will discover Charles Foster Kane." And so he sends a reporter on the quest to discover Rosebud, and that is the entire plotline of the movie. The reporter, of course, does not discover Rosebud. *We* discover Rosebud only at the end when the sled is in the furnace, and we are to conclude from this disclosure that an entire life might be defined by a single moment—when Kane as a little boy used this instrument of the sled to resist the force that was going to take him from his bucolic bliss to the world which he then began to command and mess up simultaneously. As if any life could be defined by so small a discovery. The reporter does, in fact, get to the life of Charles Foster Kane by talking to all the people who *cannot* identify Rosebud.

But it's an accident, and only a partial truth he discovers anyway. And even at the end of the movie we are not sure who Kane was, which is exactly what we were supposed to learn. Any quest that looks for the narrow answer is usually the wrong quest. Any quest that looks in the direction in which you were initially pointed is usually the wrong quest in the wrong direction. If you want to find Rosebud, look almost everywhere but at that sled and find almost everything *but* that sled.

Being out of things involves anti-specialization, and, unfortunately, we live in a world of specialization. In the most recent issue of the *Michigan Quarterly Review* someone writes, "The ego-self is being replaced by the eco-self." I wish it were true, but I do not believe it for a moment. We live in a time when specialties are becoming both stupid and dangerous. There are specialty markets, target audiences, specialty magazines like *Wood, Teeth, Aleut Life,* and so forth. But we are also living in a specialized country in which we divide ourselves among races, among regions, between sexes, and on and on. We live increasingly in a segmented world that defines itself by remorseless violence, as in the tribalism in Bosnia, or in New York, or in the Sudan, from which I have recently returned, and where I saw the work of specialists firsthand. Specialists in the north, specialists in a peculiar sect of Islamic fundamentalism specializing in "ethnic cleansing"—a high point of specialization. With sufficient specialization, eventually there will be nobody left but us, whoever the "us" is; through such specialization we live in and we will be living in a country that is the antithesis of the one that we anticipated and deserve.

Being out of things also involves avoiding the news. If anyone were interested in going into journalism I would tell him or her, "Do not read the news." I realize that is something of an encumbrance when it comes to conversations with one's employers, but there are ways that you can pick up the news secondhand.

Instead, read history, read poetry, read fiction, if you really want to understand something, if you want to get to the heart of something. We watched John McEnroe trying to make a comeback. And he would get so far and he would fall back; and he'd get a little further, and he would fall back. And you'd wonder what was happening here. People said, "Well, he's older than he was, his serve isn't as strong as it was." All the rational explanations for people who follow the news.

If you ask me, if you want to know why John McEnroe couldn't make a comeback, read Bernard Malamud's novel *The Natural.* The reason that McEnroe couldn't make a comeback is that he was a natural; he didn't believe in discipline. He couldn't work at tennis because he was so naturally good at tennis. And when all of those inborn reflexes failed him—as if he were shocked at the mismotion of his own arm, at the slowness of his own leg—then we understood John McEnroe.

The opposite of a McEnroe went to this University—the pitcher Jim Abbott, who worked and worked and worked at his craft. Abbott pitched with his left hand because he was born without a right hand. And here at Michigan he worked at and acquired the pitches that made him a star in the majors.

The nice and interesting thing about Abbott is that for all that sunny, farm-boy ordinariness about him, there is no doubt that he is eccentric too. What sort of boy at the age of five or six would look down and see emptiness at the end of his right wrist and say, "You know what I'm going to do? I'm going to be a pitcher." Naturally, he was also a quarterback. Do you want to understand what makes a pitcher? Don't worry about the physics of a curve. And surely don't read the sports pages. Read a poem by Robert Francis called "The Pitcher." It's a poem about deception. It's a poem about fooling people, which is what a pitcher does.

Do you want to understand George Bush—I don't know why you would—but if you want to understand George Bush read Ford Madox

Ford's *The Good Soldier*. Bush was a man with no center. You could tell he had no center by his use of language. Referring to Vaclav Havel, then the president of Czechoslovakia, George Bush praised Havel for having been in jail "and living and dying, whatever, for freedom."

"I think it no exaggeration," said Bush about his own election in 1988, "to say that the undecideds could go one way or the other."

I miss Bush. I hope that Larry Goldstein will forgive me for these digressions. I miss Reagan, too, for the same kind of stuff. Reagan once returned from a trip to Latin America, after which he informed us, "You know, you'd be surprised. They're all individual countries."

"Sure we made mistakes," he once said, "but point them out and we'll correct them. Let's not throw the baby out, though, with the dishes."

My favorite thing Reagan ever said is the following. The Lebanese foreign minister was giving him a half-hour lecture on all the political factions in Lebanon. *All* the political factions in Lebanon. You may imagine what this lecture sounded like. When the foreign minister concluded, Mr. Reagan approached him and said, "You know, your nose looks just like Danny Thomas's." Maybe this isn't a digression; I *am* talking about being out of things.

Being out of things involves a connection with nature. I mean a real connection with nature. We have of late, I mean of late in the last 25, 30, maybe 50 years, lost a connection with nature, and we are paying severe penalties for it.

There was a wonderful photograph I saw in a magazine a few years ago of a public demonstration by French farmers in Paris protesting against the Common Market, and they decided to make this a vivid protest by bringing in cows and sheep and slices—I forget what the technical term is—of wheat fields, so that the wheat fields could be recreated on the Champs Elysées. They put this stuff right in the middle of the city—an agrarian revolt. The police were ready for all sorts of trouble.

What happened instead was that couples started strolling through the wheat fields, and the police joined them, in a kind of visceral remembrance of something that existed in a buried life—Matthew Arnold's phrase—"the buried life." There were no clashes. The instant countryside bred companionship.

I am persuaded that the real force of the environmental movement, however other many good things will come of it, arises from a desire for our reconnection with nature. We can talk about cleaning the air, the water and oil spills, and so forth—all of which is needed. But I think the movement comes from somewhere hidden. We wish to remind ourselves of our primal connection with nature.

Being out of it involves living in the past. You remember in Thornton Wilder's play *Skin of Our Teeth* the fortune-teller says something like: "Your future? Anybody can tell you your future. I'll tell you your *past.*" Live in the past. Find the past, find *your* past. You *can* go home again. Often finding the past involves cultivating a dream state. Again, that phrase of Arnold's, "the buried life," retrieving and occupying a state of reverie. "A state of reverie does not avoid reality," said Somerset Maugham, "it accedes to reality."

Mark Twain used to curse a lot. His wife wanted to cure him of the habit. One morning his collar button was lost or something, and Twain let fly with the usual barrage: Goddamn . . . blah, blah, blah. And his wife, Livy, wanted to show him how ugly such language sounded, so she repeated verbatim what her husband had just said: Goddamn . . . blah, blah, blah. Twain stepped back, looked affectionately at his wife and said, "Livy, you know the words, but you don't know the tune." Know the tune of your life. Be out of things.

Second antirule—Be slow. All I mean by that is to wait on experience. Wait way beyond the point that you think you ought to wait before you start to create some understanding of experience, much less to make some judgment about it. Going slow is anathema for journalists, of course, who are taught to get something in as fast as possible. But it's an anathema for citizens generally, too. We pick this up, perhaps, from journalism: the need to get something fast. Get it fast. Forget it fast. Move along.

Imagine the weekend in the Politburo when the Soviet Union was still the Soviet Union and all those guys gathered together in that place, while hundreds of thousands of people in the streets of Moscow were waiting for some revelation to come out of the meeting. And the Soviet leaders emerge from that weekend, and they say to the people: "Well, from now on you can vote for a party that isn't the Communist party." After seventy years, after a single weekend, they emerge and say, "Just kidding. We really weren't serious about this Communist thing. Go about your business."

What could it mean? Every headline noted the collapse of Communism, and journalists went through the facts that traced the collapse of Communism. But what was happening here was that people realized—and what could it have meant to realize this?—that they and their parents and perhaps *their* parents, too, had been living a lie. And it was now admitted that it was a lie. And what are you supposed to do when you live a lie? I don't mean the big lie, I mean the little lies that people told to one another. The competitions for personal advancement. The lurches toward individual achievement. Any of you who visited the Soviet Union saw signs in hospitals and schools: the teacher of the week, the best worker of the week, all that stuff to reinforce the lie. And then after a single weekend the leaders say, "Well, we really didn't mean this." Vaclav Havel, so honored by President Bush, wrote an essay called "The Power of the Powerless," or "The Power of Powerlessness," in which he describes a worker in Czechoslovakia who, every day, made sure that the sign "Workers of the World Unite" stood in his window, as if he had any idea of its meaning. As if the application of it had anything to do with his life.

There was, at the time that Richard and I were at Harvard, a terribly strange story of two high school seniors who had applied to Harvard from the same high school. Let's say their names were Jones and Smith. Smith was under great pressure from his parents to go to Harvard. Nonetheless, he was rejected. Jones got into Harvard and he also got into Yale and he decided that he wanted to go to Yale, so he wrote to Harvard and said "I'm sorry. I'm not coming." Wrote to Yale and said he was coming, and went off to Yale.

Smith, knowing that Jones had done this, then wrote another letter to Harvard under Jones's name and said, "I've changed my mind. I'm coming after all." And so, Smith, under the name Jones, entered Harvard. Ordinarily you have to live in a freshman dormitory—he figured a way that he didn't have to so that he wouldn't run into people he knew. He led a life in hiding under his false name. Everything was going along fairly well for Smith, now Jones, but there is a rule applying only to the first semester, that if you get a C or below in any subject, your parents are sent a letter informing them of this. Jones, *né* Smith, was doing pretty well at Harvard, except for one course in which he got a C. Anybody, as everybody knows, can do very well at Harvard. The trick is getting in—that's the second hardest thing. The first hardest thing is being thrown out.

At any rate things were going swimmingly for our Smith, now under the name of Jones, but he got a C in one course and a note was sent home to his parents. Of course it wasn't sent home to *his* parents, it was sent home to the parents of the *real* Jones, who wrote back to Harvard saying, "We're dismayed to hear our son isn't doing too well at Harvard because he's doing quite well at Yale." Whereupon Smith/Jones was thrown out of Harvard. A minor irony in this story is that his name was expunged from the record, but of course it wasn't *his* name that was expunged from the record.

But what if he *hadn't* gotten the C, I've always wondered. That might have been the only time he could have been caught. And Smith as Jones would become Jones the sophomore. And Jones the junior. And Jones the senior. And Jones would enter law school. And Jones would get married to someone who might, if she chose to, adopt the name Jones. And their children would be called Jones and they would live a whole life named Jones. And he would die under the name Jones. And he would be buried in the cemetery, and written above his grave would be "Jones."

What does it mean to make decisions the accretion of which results in living a lie? If we knew that, we would know what happened all those decades under Communism, the meaning of those gulags, that art, those inventions, that shoe of Khrushchev's.

When I was in what was then the Soviet Union, I was taken to Latvia. Every place a visitor went in the Soviet Union, someone was attached to him who had multiple functions. He was your translator. He was your guide. And he was a spy. It was all understood, and it was all good-natured. He was also a propagandist. "We will now visit a typical Latvian fisherman," he told me. The man had been prepared for this visit for months, you know, given new clothes, a new house. "We will just drop in on him."

So, we get to this guy's house and you can see he is practically shaking. He's not prepared for any of this stuff. And meanwhile I'm told how happy all the Latvians are to be Communists and how happy it is to be fishermen in this system because you have the privilege of donating all your fish to the community fishery. And, sure enough, I would dutifully ask questions of the fisherman about his life, and he would say: "Never better, never better. I love to go out there and catch these fish and give them all to the state."

Getting nowhere in the interview, I noticed a guitar in the corner and asked simply if he played, and would he play us a folk song. He started to play, and he had the most beautiful voice. He started to sing a folk song in Latvian. And then it happened. My translator-guide-spy began to sing also, to sing thirds harmony with the fisherman in an equally beautiful voice. And for one moment, the only true moment of the day, I could understand everything that was happening there. My accompanist was, after all, Latvian. He was home. The song had brought him home. But you had to wait.

Antirule #3: Write dead stories. The rule applies to readers as well as writers. Pay attention to the stories that people forget, that they say are over. Whenever something happens there is a closure, a verdict and a trial, something that says, "You will hear no more of this." Yet the stories that reverberate in our minds, in the aftereffects of our minds, are almost always the most significant.

You may remember a story that happened in a small town in the midwest near Kansas City about twelve years ago. There was a bully in the town, I mean a really dangerous, bad-guy bully who raped women and beat up the men and was drunk all the time, and terrorized this small town. One day this guy is walking through town in the middle of the day, shots ring out, and the bully is dead. Cops come in and ask who did it. Beats me, says the town, didn't see a thing. Middle of the day, small town, everybody knew who shot this guy, but nobody saw a thing. Maybe there were several who shot him.

The cops give up. Federal agents come in, as in the Rodney King case. They decide, "Well, if we can't get anywhere with this as a murder case, we can decide that the man was deprived of his civil rights." There is a kind of logic to that. When you are killed, you really are deprived of your civil rights. Feds go in there, the town clams up just as it did before. Nope, didn't see a thing. Nothing.

For twelve years no one in that town has said a word in public about what happened on that Saturday afternoon. But imagine the story now. Now the dead man is no longer a bully. He's dead twelve years. And the town, meanwhile, has been living with a conspiracy, with the common knowledge that one or more among them is capable of murder. And this is a secret they cannot divulge. If you want a story, don't worry about the bully. Go into the town now, if you dare.

In New York a couple of years ago there was a terrible incident involving a man named Rodney Sumpter, who, being menaced by a homeless man in a subway—Rodney Sumpter was with his child—leapt upon the homeless man and beat him to death; beat his head against the subway platform. There was no indictment, and *that* case was over. It was in several ways a dead story. But why did that story reverberate in the minds of New Yorkers and in the minds of those who would read the story outside New York? Because it involved the inarticulate, unexpressed rage at the impotence people everywhere feel about homelessness. The admixture of fear and pity. Of wanting to do something to correct what you know is wrong, and not being able to. All the feelings that New Yorkers have as they step gingerly over the bodies of their fellow creatures on their way to work; they were in that story. Yet it was a dead story; there was no indictment. Nothing is ever over. The mind lives in aftereffects.

Antirule #4: Go to hell. What I mean by that is simply something you writers in the audience know already. You discover chaos inside you. It is useful. Use it. Nietzsche said, "You must have chaos within you to give birth to a dancing star." I mean discover real chaos. The kind of chaos that Huck Finn discovered when he decided to go to hell to do something honorable. Where I live there is chaos everywhere. I look out my window on Broadway and see chaos performing. What reverberates in me is the same chaos. Go to hell. It is useful.

Antirule #5: Distrust rational thought. We know the value of rational thought. We ought to be more in tune with the instruction of irrational thought, of intuition. We see public figures about whom we know something is terribly wrong, but we listen to the evidence and the words, and we decide to make definitions about those figures according to the externalities. You see Bud McFarland testify in the Iran-Contra investigation. You feel something is terribly wrong with him, and then something actually goes wrong; he tries to kill himself. Your intuition was right. Bess Myerson is picked up for shoplifting. All you had to do was trust your intuition. Oliver North with all that stolid talk, and that solid stance. Is there doubt in anybody's mind that he is crazy as a loon?

I work with some friends in my neighborhood with a homeless group. We do very little—put out a journal once a month consisting of the stories of their lives. We interview them, and then we write their stories, on the idea, which seems to work, that seeing their lives in print gives them a kind of credibility, puts them back on earth.

In one of these interviews I said to a woman named Betty, a woman in her sixties, "Betty, can I talk to you about your life?" She said, "Oh, I'd like to talk to you, Roger, but CBS is coming over later to interview me, so I don't know how much time I have. And you know how it is when you've been a former showgirl and Miss America and you've had all this celebrity and you've had a Hollywood screen test, and you've dated Joe DiMaggio. But if I have the time, I'll talk to you." So I wrote up what she told me, but I asked the psychiatrist in charge of the place if there was any harm in recording these fantasies. He said not if Betty believed them herself.

Two weeks before Betty died peacefully in her sleep a young woman came looking for her, who turned out to be her daughter, born in a mental institution in Texas where Betty had been a patient. The daughter in her dogged search for her mother had gone from state to state, and had finally come to our neighborhood and found her mother, and they were reunited. It was miraculous for the couple of weeks of life left to Betty.

The daughter also carried with her evidence that everything Betty had told me was true. She *had* been a showgirl in the Latin Quarter nightclub. She was not Miss America, but she was Miss Ohio, and she had gone to the Miss America contest. Another fact she *didn't* mention was that her brother was a pitcher for the Cincinnati Reds. She *did* date Joe DiMaggio, and she had a Hollywood screen test.

If I had been looking where I ought to have been looking, I would have believed all that about Betty, but I was trusting what seemed to be reasonable, rational thought. You see, Betty sang in the streets. If you listened to the voice, even through all that cigarette smoke, there was the truth about Betty—in her songs. Shelley said, "We need the power to imagine what we know." (That quotation, by the way, was taught to me this morning by Larry Goldstein, my closest friend.)

Antirule #6: Be beside the point. It's a variation of being out of things, but with a specific direction. It means literally choosing the other direction. I'm going to begin with a basketball anecdote, though I realize basketball is a painful subject to raise here at Michigan after the NCAA finals.

The basketball anecdote about looking the other way has to do with a back-court man at the University of Arkansas who was not doing so well, and he asked his coach what he was doing wrong. The coach said, "What do you do in practice?"

The kid answered, "I dribble and shoot, like most people."

The coach said, "In the next full scrimmage game, have somebody clock how much time you actually have your hands on the ball. That is, whether you're dribbling or you're shooting."

The kid did that, came back, and the coach asked, "How much

time was it?" The kid was the point guard, so he would have his hands on the ball more time than other players. He reported that the time he handled the ball came to something over two minutes. A little over two minutes—out of forty. The player was shocked, of course. The coach asked, "What do you learn from that?"

The kid said, "I don't know."

The coach said, "Most of the game is played away from the ball." In journalism, in the things that we watch, in the life we observe, most of the game is played away from the ball. Journalists are taught to be like heliotropic plants, to turn where the light is, or to turn where the noise is. But if you want to know about something, I mean really know about something, look away from the ball. If you want to know about poverty, don't look at a march on Washington, or at a tenement fire. Study the poor all the time. The poor are poor all the time.

Every time there is a natural disaster—the Ohio flood, the hurricane in Florida—people are missing the point by being on the point. So we are always told about these events in terms of the millions of dollars lost or how many people were injured, property damage, and so forth . . . when what we know to be the deeper truth, the inner life, the buried life of the story, is that we are helpless in nature still, and that nothing prepares us for certain events no matter how "advanced" we are. As we develop invention after invention, and sophistication after sophistication, these inexplicable uncontrollable things will always occur. *That* is the story of natural disasters.

Look away from the ball. Study people in repose, not people in crisis. There is a myth that exists among writers that behavior in the critical moment will reveal character. I do not believe it. I believe that behavior in the critical moment merely reveals behavior in the critical moment. And that people behave in aberrant ways in crises. But study people in repose, and you might have a chance of knowing what is going on inside their minds.

Antirule #7: Avoid the company of people. I regard that as an excellent general rule, but I will apply it to this talk as well. What I mean by this is to cultivate a useful privacy. There is so little privacy in our world, and again, as with the separation from nature, we are paying penalties for it. Rousseau said, "If I had to choose my place of birth, I would have chosen a state in which everyone knew everyone else so that neither the obscure tactics of vice nor the modesty of virtue could have escaped public scrutiny and judgment." Rousseau is what one would call in French a *tête* case. Who in his right mind would want a society where everything that one did or thought would be available to public scrutiny and judgment?

What purpose was served by revealing Arthur Ashe's AIDS? What good was served, except to provoke an extra amount of pain in a man who was going to die anyway, for those last months of his life? And it is not just that privacy is invaded in our time. Privacy is surrendered willingly—surrendered on Oprah, on Geraldo, on Donahue. I am always dumbstruck to watch the parents of children killed in a crossfire able to talk to a television reporter moments afterwards with all the aplomb of a seasoned television performer. They are ready to be public figures, ready to give out.

I don't really mean to advocate avoiding the company of people as much as I mean husbanding your time so that you are aware of the value of yourself without stumbling over into egocentricity or selfishness. I go back to Wordsworth. Coleridge was said to have visited Wordsworth, gone into the cottage, stayed four or five hours. They didn't say a word to each other. As Coleridge was walking out the door, he thanked Wordsworth for a perfect evening.

What privacy does is to develop certain valuable things in you. It develops a sense of language, of real language, not false language, not public language. For you, prize winners in these writing contests, the development of private language is essential. You will be misled. There will be temptations all the time to use some other word that is not your word.

So many words are used oddly today. I hear the word "fun" in the craziest contexts. A man works twenty years composing a dictionary of Zoroastrianism. Asked how the project went, he said "It was fun." An actor appears in a one-man play, *Pol Pot Tonight*. Says it was "fun," it was a lot of "fun."

There is a product advertised on late-night television in New York called "Safe Ears." A woman steps forward to advertise gold-looking earrings that contain condoms inside. Condoms hidden in the earrings. Most inventive. The world has certainly come a long way from the Roy Rogers bullet ring I had as a boy, with its secret compartment, which contained nothing. Something else about "Safe Ears." They sell three to a set. Three earrings to a set. You'd think if your date was so constructed as to be able to wear three earrings, safe sex would be the least of her concerns. But the woman steps forward to say, "Safe ears are fabulous. And *fun.*"

Cultivate privacy because private thoughts are much more complicated than public thoughts. It has to do, again, with this chaos within you. Think of the way the mind is most of the time. This roiling of words. All this chaos which then comes out in some orderly fakery we call conversation. But the state of mind before that moment; that's the thing to cultivate. That is the private self.

Most of all, privacy, oddly enough, makes the best social sense. I think civilizations are made up of interacting privacies. That's where people really learn community; to be with one another. A sense of self, and then a sense of other, in that order.

The eighth antirule: "Betray your sources." I don't mean this the way it sounds. If somebody tells you a secret you don't say who it was. I mean something far colder. Every journalist deliberately betrays the people he or she interviews. The act is justified in the name of a larger truth, but it is still a betrayal.

The most extravagant experience I had with betrayal was with Richard Nixon. I interviewed him twice. The first time I put my tape recorder beside him. He looked at it—true story—and said, "Oh, that's one of those new tape recorders. They are so much better than the old tape recorders." I did not know if he was joking. I did not laugh. I did not say, "Oh, yes, Mr. President, these don't skip a minute." I did not say that.

I was interviewing him for a story I was doing on the anniversary of Hiroshima and I wanted to talk to somebody who had had his finger on or near the button more than anyone else, and Nixon qualified. The story came out; Nixon was delighted. I wasn't interested in Watergate for the story. I made no comments about his character or about his leaving office or anything. I was interested in Nixon as nuclear diplomat, and he was very knowledgeable on this subject. So we became pen pals in a sense. He would send me notes from time to time. I thought that this was a unique distinction until I discovered that he was sending hundreds of people in my profession notes, all for the same purpose—redeeming his name.

Then I was asked by *Time* to write a profile of Nixon. I did, and do, think he is the most interesting political character in my lifetime, and I was glad to write about him. I wrote a scathing profile. It was called

"The Dark Comedian" and I just let fly with all the contempt that I held for what he did to the highest office in the country. Nixon flew off the handle, wrote to *Time* saying, "I will not give an interview to any organization in which Rosenblatt is working." His timing was poor, because in that particular summer I was working for *Time,* MacNeil/Lehrer, and CBS.

Of course, he didn't mean any of this. The thing that got him sore was the thought that I had betrayed him, and of course I had. In the interview he granted for this profile, I showed no sign that I was about to tell the world what I thought of Richard Nixon. I did my very best to let Nixon be Nixon, and to say all the things I wanted him to say, without misrepresenting what he was saying, in order to enact a work of obvious, blatant betrayal in the name of something else, of some other loyalty.

Yet did I understand Nixon? Do I understand Nixon now? No. It was and is all beyond me.

And so, I come to the ninth and last, and to me, the guiding antirule—Do not understand it. I do not mean pretend not to understand it and then create some other fiction within the fiction. I mean do not understand it. Retain the mystery.

I was watching the Academy Awards a couple of years ago. Typical ceremony: the most glittery people in the world, dressed to the nines. Dazzling. I had the remote control and I turned to the news, on which they showed the bodies lined up in that Bronx Happyland Social Club fire of the same year. The bodies were awaiting burial. I thought: How can I be seeing these two things almost simultaneously? Will they, said the mind trying to make connections, make a movie of the Happyland fire some day? Will it win an Academy Award?

I came back recently from a trip to the Sudan where I saw the worst place in the world. There is no second place. I've seen places where, physically, things were worse. But what makes Sudan the most heartbreaking place I have ever seen is that while people are dying from intratribal war, and the ethnic cleansing by the Moslems in the north of the Christians and animists in the south, while they are dying of all the diseases attributed to starvation and malnutrition, the thing that makes the Sudan the worst place I have ever seen is that nobody cares. Nobody is doing anything about it.

How can what is happening in the Sudan exist in the same world in which we, now, look at one another in this gracious hall, in which we take pleasure in one another's existence, wish one another the best? George Steiner in *Language and Silence* asks, "How could I be going to the movies and making love in New York at the same time that children were being dumped into the ovens in Auschwitz?" It is beyond us. I do not understand it. Do not understand it.

From that lack of understanding comes the kind of awe of experience out of which our work as writers could do a little good, could have its reverberations in other souls. Do not understand Rosebud.

When I was in high school, my father took me to the play *Inherit the Wind*. It starred Paul Muni playing the role of Clarence Darrow, and Ed Begley (Ed Begley, *Sr.*, you have to say now) in the role of William Jennings Bryan. And it introduced a new actor, Tony Randall, in the role of a character called Hornbeck who was to represent H. L. Mencken. You know the story of *Inherit the Wind;* it's the Scopes "monkey trial" in Tennessee where the teacher was tried for teaching evolution, and lost the case, but won the point.

I was sitting there with my father, having no knowledge that I would ever enter journalism, wanting to be a writer but not knowing how that was ever going to be achieved. In the middle of the play, the Bryan character has a stroke. He has a stroke because he is overwhelmed by the idea that he is defending the indefensible, and as eloquent as he is, he can't take it. And Hornbeck, the journalist, regards this as Darrow's triumph. Darrow has been brilliantly rational throughout on the matter of evolution, and the two of them, the journalist and Darrow, are on the stage together. The journalist gloats and says to Darrow, "Well, you really got him! You really made a fool of that Bible-beating bastard!"

And Darrow, heaving with contempt, looks at the journalist and says, "What could a man like you possibly know about a man like that?"

That is our question.

Writers and Their Characters

Geoffrey Wolff

Some invitations you don't regret. This is one. The previous offer too tempting to decline came from a Moroccan school that asked me to say a little speech at last June's graduation. My son was teaching there, at the American School of Tangier, and cynics might remark with raised eyebrows that my invitation came as a product of nepotism. I hope cynics, for once, were right. I'd be gratified to imagine that my son pulled strings to get me invited across an ocean to his school to talk for fifteen minutes. If he did, he didn't pull very hard, because there was no payday—what we artists have learned to term "a modest honorarium"—attached to my performance. Moreover, news that shriveled my spirit, there would be—as ever at such ceremonies—a prize-giving.

I had sat through high school Prize Days and these were not my happiest memories. Not that I haven't received my due portion of superlatives: if my school yearbook voted my best friend "Smartest," classmates voted me "Thinks He Is." My school headmaster, searching for a perfect absolute to apply to my ambitious self, dubbed me The Weak Link in an Otherwise Strong Choate Chain. Later I cleaned up my act, learned to play the game. That is, to be honored and be-ribboned at Prize Day, I learned to sell out; this was bravura selling-out. I was at boarding school for a year in England. Because my fellow students were conspicuously better-educated than I was, smoother writers, quicker at Latin and whatnot, more deft at rugby and cricket, I set my cap on the one school prize that just might have my name on it. To win the Brian Tunstall Imperial Studies Prize an essay on a set subject was required; that year the subject was The American Rebellion of 1776: Why and How. This was not a magnet to my fellow students; I saw hope here. All I had to do was sell out my country, make snide references to the colony's pathetic "peasant citizenry," its bumpkin stubbornness, the short-sightedness that led by awful degrees to a nation of

---

The Hopwood Lecture, 1994

oafish automobilists so ignorant that they drive on the wrong side of the road. I stand before you the recipient of Eastbourne College's Brian Tunstall Imperial Studies Prize in the year 1956, an award that consisted of the gift of a book, *The Seven Pillars of Wisdom,* just the thing for a fan of empire and an apprentice traitor.

I've come to dread the spring, all those announcements of The Best This, Most Distinguished That. It doesn't help that these awards are dealt out during Academy Award season, not to mention the NCAA basketball playoffs. Who lost, who called the time-out that wasn't, who sits sweating it out under the lights at Dorothy Chandler Pavilion wearing a ridiculous dress or dinner jacket, trying to paint a brave smile on her perfect face, his perfect face, clapping like a trained seal when some paltry upstart wins Best Supporting Actress even though the loser *knows* she's a better actress because she's doing such a perfect job of playing the part of a smiling good sport.

Something evil kicks in at Prize Days. An urge to give the teacher's pet a noogie in the playground. So imagine my pleasure at The American School of Tangier when I saw that serious prizes are bestowed only on students in pre-kindergarten through third grade: Omar Kebdani was given a tricycle for being "a cheerful boy who has contributed to a happy attitude" in pre-kindergarten. For her "sweet nature" in kindergarten Zarah Scullion got a bicycle with training wheels. For her "charming personality" in second grade, a bicycle without training wheels was given to Ines Doval.

When Robert Kennedy was alive, that most competitive man and his family hosted an annual pet show. Only blue ribbons were bestowed. Handsomest Goldfish With a Bitten Dorsal; Most Serene Fifteen Year Old Irish Setter; Best Behaved Turtle, Slowest Turtle, Best-Hidden Turtle. Every entrant went home a winner and this was as it should have been. *Every* writer who shows up for the contest and stays till the end deserves a blue ribbon. I mean this. What writers do is hard, deserves to be honored.

I could say it doesn't count who wins or loses, that it matters only how we play the game. That is, I could be a homiletic fool. Let me spare you. The American practice of ranking is too durable to surrender to mere cliché. The myth of eternal progress dies hard here, and its calculus leads inexorably to a faith in Numero Uno. I recall watching an extraordinary NBA championship game between the Lakers and my beloved Celtics, Bird contending with Magic. It was an inspired contest and the playing of it brought awed goofy grins to the opposing players even after the game ended. Of course there was a winner and a loser (never mind which was which), but believe it or not the players at first didn't seem to notice that there had been a final result to their play, until the chant cascaded down from the bleachers: "We're Number One!" Victorious pitlings waved those grotesque foam rubber idiot fingers at defeated pitlings: "We're Number One!"

This is the mentality, the writer as prize fighter, Hemingway imagining himself in the ring against Tolstoy, Mailer versus Hem, that gives score-keeping a bad name. It elevates outcome over process, career over calling, publication over writing. It's as simplistic as a thumb up or thumb down, Siskel & Ebertry, two dumb thumbs turned either which way. It encourages a coarse taxonomy—this champeen is one of the five best epic poets writing since the Korean War, that one the best novelist ever to win the Brian Tunstall Imperial Studies Prize in 1956.

The habit of ranking is epidemic in our country. Its most vulgar expression is ten-best lists, who's on the short list, who's been cut. Discrimination can be delicate or gross, the practice of learning to select and exclude clothes, college applicants, clubmates, friends, lovers. Of course, not all discrimination is unwholesome. For a writer exclusion and selection exhibit themselves word upon word: this word is better than that word but here—behold!—the last *best* word. And for a writer there's an even more complicated aspect to discrimination; I speak of the mysterious program by which we are chosen by our passions, our obsessions, that series of choices that provokes us to tell this story rather than that story.

But how do any of us license ourselves to tell any story at all, and why should anyone listen, let alone turn a thumb up, tack a blue ribbon to the title page? Writers, when they finally find their voices, are shrewdly guarded, uncomfortable with anyone who knew them back when, back before they could sing, back when they could merely yawp and bark and whine. Juvenilia ain't a pretty sight or for sure a pretty sound. In fact, the phenomenon of youthful stylistic gracelessness is so inevitable a fact of every writer's experience that many ripe writers recollect their early careers with shame, others with amusement, all with a sense of disconnection from that prehistoric self. No writer who owned copy paper and a file cabinet can pretend to be ignorant of the awkward truth of his or her beginnings, of the early self's bumptious posturing, misdirected attention, unfelt passion and unearned contempt.

And because I can read now what I wrote then, I know that the wickedest and stupidest mischief any teacher of writing can commit against a student of writing is to tell that student—on *any* provocation or botched attempt—that that student is without hope, that that student should shut up.

I suspect that like most fiction writers in this room I began composing stories on the page after I had given myself a creative writing workshop by telling lies to pals in the school cafeteria and to strangers on trains. For reasons both sound and meretricious the life I was living during adolescence was insufficient to my ignoble ambitions and to my nobler dreams. I made up a new life—new lives—for myself. Because I soon became lonely in that meagerly populated alternate world, inhabited only by people who shared my passionate preoccupation with me, time came when I peopled it with men and women—boys and girls, then—who had their own imperatives, who chafed against their own deficient destinies. I tried, that is, to make characters. Looking back now at those makings and unmakings, I flinch. I blush. To play God is to give oneself a license; I chose back then to remain ignorant of the responsibility that comes with liberty. I mean that the world I invented for others was often reflexively mean; my people too often were mean also, outlandishly costumed, moronic, goitered, foolish, errant, too fat, too skinny, too baldheaded, too near-sighted, too horny, too easy to laugh at.

Why, I wonder now? The simple answer is that such characters demand less art, less complication, in the making. In her explanation of her methods, that virtuoso of the grotesque Flannery O'Connor justifies her exaggeration of her characters by observing that "to the hard of hearing you shout, and for the almost blind you draw large and startling figures." Of course O'Connor was attempting to imitate for the disbelieving or uncertain reader the movements of faith, what she took to be the experience of grace, the human-scaled adventure of epiphany. I, by contrast, was playing for a laugh, printing portraits on high-contrast paper so they'd be easy to see at a quick glance, being as easy on myself as I was hard on my characters.

It's tempting now to disavow what I made in my apprentice years as a novelist. I say "apprentice years as a novelist" so casually: I'm referring offhand to eight years of writing fiction, laboring daily on three novels now out of print. I'm happy enough to have them out of print, but I'm also mindful that auto-Schadenfreude, a smirking derision for one's earlier self, has become a besetting vice of middle-aged writers. An awful shrewdness motivates this pervasive disloyalty to our earlier selves. In a recent story, "Smorgasbord," my dear brother Tobias causes his narrator, looking back on the foolish energy and treachery and deforming outcome of adolescent love, to meditate:

> We're supposed to smile at the passions of the young, and at what we recall of our own passions, as if they were no more than a series of sweet frauds we had fooled ourselves with and then wised up to. Not only the passion of boys and girls for each other but the others, too—passion for justice, for doing right, for turning the world around—all these come in their time under our wintry smiles. But there was nothing foolish about what we felt. Nothing merely young.

Toby is contemplating youthful romance, and I am contemplating youthful distemper, but I hope I'm right in ascribing both kinds of expression to passion. It is wrong to repudiate wholesale those earlier turmoils of the spirit. Stanley Kunitz has offered an opinion, following the experience of reviewing his life's work for a collection of poems, that writers don't evolve, they change. Not *merely* change, of course: style, after all is character, and character style, so that changes in a writer's preoccupations, a writer's attitude toward his created characters, have the deepest consequence. But it is true that to get to here, we leave there; for every piece of new ground we take, we abandon a position. To achieve the serenity I wish for my characters I have neglected perturbation, gaining compassion I have defused ferocity. And worst fear of all, I have taken to looking over my shoulder at my readers and critics. Once I wanted to make noise. This expressed itself as foolishly as farting in chapel or as strenuously as shouting in outrage. Now, I fear, I've learned to mind my manners. Wouldn't it be awful to discover, looking in the mirror at my bald head and white beard, after all this I've learned to be . . . what? A good boy? The Strong Link in an Otherwise Weak Choate Chain?

Critics like to prattle about writers' gifts and promise. Promise is a sham; promise implies a debt, and no writer owes anyone anything, unless that writer chooses to owe himself or herself a shot at finding a voice. Gift is a fantasy; late at night or (better) at the cusp of dawn, with Coltrane or Monk or Miles sneaking sweetly out of the speakers, the prose writers who are my friends will confess that gift is an illusion, a magic trick learned by practice. None of us was born with teeth and beard and word processor. I believe that the only gift any writer can hope to hold is the gift of character, and that good character—generosity and engagement—is not a pre-existent quality that a good person brings to his or her work, by blind genetic luck. I believe that good character is created by good work. And good work in its turn is generous work. I'm not referring to "moral fiction," whatever John Gardner may have meant by that honorific. I mean a world populated by human beings who are not just one thing, not just another. I'm speaking of characters unbounded by a writer's narrow plan for them and use of them. Characters who can be blue on Monday morning and full of song that night. Characters who can do some monstrous deed—shoot a bank teller, make love to a younger sister maybe even feeling love for her—and then perform a kindness, dry the dishes, comfort a friend.

If writing is done a word at a time, so it is read a word at a time, and its value—if it has any—comes from just this, a consecutive and manifest record of choices made, *in the moment,* now, a process rather than an outcome. Those choices make then a personal history of choices, a big mosaic made of tiny pieces, the letters of the alphabet, marks of punctuation as tiny as periods. Writing has nothing to do with what is going to happen—a movie sale, a National Book Award; it has everything to do with what is happening. Choosing words laboriously one at a time—with false starts and every imaginable mistake and then, in the face of awful discouragements, repairing with grunt labor what is broken or deformed—answering this calling one learns, *must* understand, that the failure of a word, sentence, story, novel is not prophetic. From all the opportunities to get it wrong, even to do wrong on the page, one learns, glacially, that it *is* possible to get there from here. This, together with the odd truth that for a writer bad luck (an unhappy childhood, say) can be translated into the good luck of a good story, is as close as I have come to experiencing faith in alchemy, in a perpetual motion machine, in a free lunch.

I don't want to deform the integrity of these experiences by casual sermonizing. It is daunting for any writer of good will to know how to express his or her better angels. Take stamina, putatively the most accessible aspect of a writer's good character. The third and last of those early novels to which I referred above is *Inklings,* begun in 1971 under the pressure of desperation. Following the publication of my first novel. *Bad Debts,* which like most first novels came fast and happily, which like many first novels was greeted warmly by reviewers, probably from the same critical reflex that provokes an audience of parents to give a standing ovation to an elementary school performance of *Macbeth,* I had caught a bad case of *I-wrote-a-book disease.* I finished a second novel, quit a job at Princeton, quit a job at *Newsweek,* cashed out a small pension, took my wife and young sons to Brittany. The idea was simple: we would live off the advance I got for my second novel, *The Sightseer.* That there was to be such an advance was, I was certain, a done deal. The then editor of one of America's more prestigious publishing companies had told me after reading my first novel that he would publish anything I gave him. I gave him, weeks before we left for France and after I had quit my day jobs, *The Sightseer.* Mr. Gottlieb's response: "I meant I'd publish anything but this."

It was time to regroup. I now had a drug-resistant case of *I've-written-a-rejected-book disease,* also known as second novel disease, only known cure—start a third. So I did, and thereupon embarked on a five year serial remedy of submission (what a word!) and revision (what a concept!). I lifted a heavy soul to the writing loft those years, would not abandon my two darlings, saw them through thin and thin. Got them, by Jove, *published* (in such measly numbers that unsigned copies of *The Sightseer* and *Inklings* are more valuable, rarer too, than the inscribed books). My regret here is not owing, I hope and believe, to meager sales. I worked on *Inklings* all the way up to 1976, long after I'd ceased to be caught in its net, long after I'd ceased really to care about it. I understood this to be good character, forbearance, tenacity, grit, fidelity. Today I think this was a mistake, or it wasn't; I learned from it; *Inklings* was a whole graduate school in pain and error. Finally, after eight years, now vee may perhaps to begin? Back then this is what I believed: I was a writer; I had to write, right? It was promised; I was promised.

In the end writing is a contest. The conflict is against one's lesser self. One sovereign expression of this competition is the writer's attitude toward his or her characters. I would like to believe that everything we need to know about a writer's character—stamina, good faith, curiosity, warmth, unsolemn seriousness, compassion—is expressed through that crucial relationship between the writer and the writer's invented creatures. Stanley Elkin has written that writing is a revenge against bullies. It levels the playing field for geeks, unlocks the gate for outsiders, evens the odds. To create characters for whom a writer feels indifference or contempt is to be a bully oneself.

Why would anyone want to take the trouble to conjure up a fish, equip the creature with fins and gills, color the scales pretty, invent for this fish a sea to swim in but limit that sea to a littoral bound by a barrel, and all this ado of creation merely to shoot the damned fish? Writers do it all the time, inseminate and give birth to characters merely to mock them, box their ears, bring them low. But why?

Maybe from a sourness born of self-pity. So much is stacked against the writer: neglect, solipsism, a miserable hourly wage, envy, despair. Where writers gather there they share the oral history, the low comedy of tribal lore: the humiliations of barding around, the megalomania of fellow writers, the logrolling of blurbologists, the perfidy of editors, the signed copy of one's book discovered by the writer for sale at the Strand the day after it has been given as a gift. One hears of the book printed by Doubleday and sent by a miracle of automation directly to the shredder, without taking a detour to warehouse and bookstore. It's enough to make you weep, or turn you into a cynic, or make you hard on your characters.

There are so many ways to make a wrong narrative turn: using close third person voice a writer can step too hard on a character's neck, outshout him, drown out his voice with your own. In first person a writer can miscalculate proportion, miscalibrate a reader's willingness to sympathize with a narrator's predicament. In deference to the ugly imperatives of self-interest, with mad fidelity to narrative self-focus, a writer can decide to let his character complain aloud of toothache while she's bedside in a cancer ward. Such recklessness can be foolhardy, grotesque. Yet without the courage to pursue a character's character down the dark alleys where will *will* lead, the writer surrenders to feeble and unfelt piety, as though Iago were to say, Gee, I'm sorry, as though Richard III were to cry, My kingdom! Take it, you deserve it.

Norman Mailer, in a *Paris Review* interview, was asked "what can ruin a first-rate writer?" His reply was not inclusive, but it spelunked the major caves: "Booze, pot, too much sex, too much failure in one's private life, too much attrition, too much recognition, too little recognition, frustration. Nearly everything in the scheme of things works to dull a first-rate talent. But the worst probably is cowardice—as one gets older, one becomes aware of one's cowardice, the desire to be bold which once was a joy gets heavy with caution and duty. And finally there's apathy."

Mailer's right. Writing is difficult. Not harder than anything; not harder than stripping asbestos or digging post-holes in the rain or jackhammering asphalt under a hot sun or nursing the sick. Not hard like dancing topless or selling religion door-to-door. Writing is more like playing acoustic guitar on the makeshift stage of a concrete-block roadhouse in competition with a really quite challenging pinball machine; let's agree the work is difficult. Dark and lonely, and nobody has to do it.

If ever you need a definition of a discretionary use of time, fiction writing and reading will fill the bill. If one Sunday the newspapers had no new novel to review, eyebrows might be raised. The next Sunday, same empty story, same blank pages, no new novels, an atmosphere of anxiety. Sunday after that, think pieces: Whither Literature? It's a nice fantasy, like imagining how dearly we'll be missed after we die. Writers are one-by-oners, one-at-a-timers, bespoke tailors. We don't write to fill a quota of books, and so we know very well, hurtfully well, how well the world can get by without this one particular thing we are each, in mad solitude, trying to tailor-make. *Non serviam* cuts both ways. *So what? is* a question I have asked and asked and asked my work. And this too is why my cottage industry is difficult. Unrequited love's a stone terror. It was so in 4th Grade, it is so on publication day. There's the book, an ad in the Personals. *Comely, comic, complex, comprehensible.* Writer looking for reader, long-term relationship wanted. Writing's a preposterous enterprise, crazy lonely and then crazy public. Squirreled away squirrely at your damned desk however many years, and then naked in the crosshairs of a reader or a reviewer's spectacles, if you're lucky. It's such a tricky business, this blind date, a writer and reader.

So let's agree writing isn't easy. Life isn't easy. And we shouldn't make what is difficult for all of us more difficult for our own newborn, for our characters let's say. Diminishing them, robbing them of language, failing to feel with their senses, turning our backs on them. I believe that a creative life, a life of which it might be possible to be proud, begins with the simple act of meaning one's characters well, of giving them their best shot at life, language, and the pursuit of energy.

Writers are first-class complainers, wonderful whiners, bravura bellyachers and—great grief!—great grievers. I don't believe of course that woe is exclusively us, that sorrow, rue, and ire are peculiar to writers, that some genetic glitch has soured our temperaments, exacerbated our exquisite sense of injury. It isn't writers' essential natures that so reflexively sour our pusses; it's our amplifying profession, the broadcast of our gloom, its publication.

So what's our gripe? That we're inadequately loved, of course, by which writers at their pettiest mean inappreciatively reviewed, carelessly read, insufficiently read. In fact, it's an extraordinary union, the collision between a writer and a reader. All that competing noise out there, all that sound and fury, all those words. And a writer, a perfect stranger—oh, a most imperfect stranger!—cries out to a fellow stranger, "Stop what you're doing. Fish some other morning, plant bulbs next weekend. Read me. Shut up and pay close attention, now, hear me out—hear only me."

And it happens. The preposterous claim on your undivided attention we writers pray you'll honor—some of you, sometimes, honor it. Maybe not a Rose Bowl full, but some of you, enough to make a quorum, put together a nice party.

This is a nice party, a gathering of the tribes. So in honor of the occasion and for all of you writers out there at the beginning or in the middle of things, of this life we share—take it from me: you take the prize.

The Writer as a Character

Diane Johnson

It's a particular pleasure to be here, because Ann Arbor has always been a place of legend to me. I am the sister and daughter of University of Michigan alumni, but I have never visited the campus. Over the years I have had several friends who received Hopwood prizes—a few days ago I had lunch with Edmund White, my neighbor in Paris. I don't know when I have read a book as avidly as Nicholas Delbanco's anthology of former Hopwood lectures, *Speaking of Writing.* Writers in America, dispersed as we are, starve for shop-talk, and this collection is like having a wonderful conversation about literature with an impressive and admired group of predecessors on this podium.

When I was done reading it, I had a lot of "how true's" in the margin, not to mention "but ifs." I might have taken as my text Norman Mailer's observation that "Experience when it cannot be communicated to another must wither within and be worse than lost." How true, though maybe only true for writers? That is, for people who must write, as compared to people who want to lead a writer's life. Creative writing classes are full of both types, often equally talented; but the latter usually don't end up being writers, perhaps because they don't have the writer's sort of character. My subject I could describe as being the writer's character as desired by the reader, and revealed in the old-fashioned elements of the narrative—plot, style, and subject—coincidentally the very narrative elements Saul Bellow said in his Hopwood lecture of 1961 were finished. Bellow especially attacked "the badly faded ideas of motives and drama or love and hate" as being possibly only of interest to clinical psychologists and sociologists. That was very much in the Freud-dominated spirit of the time, and things were to get worse for the old-fashioned art of story-telling, which I would like to offer a little defense of today.

By chance, on my way here, something happened that exactly

The Hopwood Lecture, 1995

illustrates my theme. I was in the airport bookshop. It might as well have been called the Danielle Steele bookshop, completely lined from floor to ceiling and wall to wall with books by this popular author. A woman wondering at the vast array of alluring titles asked the bookshop lady "but which one?" "Oh, it doesn't matter," said the bookstore lady. "They're all Steeles." This in turn reminded me of a few years ago, when I was one of several writers on a program, one of whom was Louis L'Amour, the writer of western novels, with an audience of four thousand attentive listeners who to a person lined up afterward to get L'Amour's signature on their old copies of his books. Yet, I now discover, few readers can mention the titles or any of the characters or recount the plots of L'Amour's or Steele's novels, let alone quote a line. The qualities that drew these readers were inherent in the writers, not in the works, some resonance of sensibility.

I wish I could announce that I was here going to reveal the secret of selling millions of copies of novels. Alas. But I do want to say something about the neglected subject of the writer herself, himself, in his pages, carrying over from book to book. The author, not the narrator. I mean the sense we have as we read there are three of us involved—ourself, the narrator, and the writer. Reading *Huckleberry Finn,* there are Huck and I, and Mark Twain, and as I read, I address certain thoughts to Twain, no matter how scarce he makes himself, hiding behind Huck. As readers I think we always have a sense of an author's presence, alive in her text, looking over our shoulder as we read, and we have an affection for one author over another; and there's the fact that though we will read about characters we don't like, we don't read a writer whom we don't like. The practical implication of this for us as writers is that it is ourselves, finally, that have to stand up to some serious tests of not only talent and industry but character, commitment, and what Henry James called, rather dauntingly, "quality of mind."

I should say again that I'm talking about the writer as distinct from the narrator. In an allegory painting of narrative fiction, the narrator would be the Madonna or saint in the middle of the picture, and the writer would be the God-like figure behind, up in the sky, with golden rays of force emitting from his forehead or fingers. There is of course one thing particularly medieval and naive about the painting—the unfashionable figure of God. God is not represented in modern painting, just as the writer is no longer admitted into his narrative except as subject. It is in part the direction all art has gone, from naive allegory to abstract expressionism. Flaubert decreed that the author should be "nowhere apparent." Roland Barthes in 1968 took a harder line; as an "institution the author is dead." The irrelevance of the writer to the literary project, the death of the writer, was announced somewhat after the death of God, but the two demises are not unrelated, I think, and are part of a general modern political dynamic, pushing from the left to devalue or challenge authority of any kind, terrorizing on the right with death threats for authorial transgressions.

Serious critics from Michigan or Yale have by now abandoned speaking of the writer at all. Once he has performed his unwitting creative part, we are told to forget about him and his intentions in the work, his need for money in the winter of 1942, his lifelong obsession for frogs—the text must stand for itself. The worst of this is that writers have tended to accept the death of the writer too. I think as American writers we have shrunk from our readers. This may sound odd in a time when people write about themselves obsessively, with a kind of unstoppable reflex candor—we are so good at "sharing" our feelings. Europeans say American friendliness is our disguise, our candor a mask behind which, because we omit knowable social rites, we are unknowable. The first-person, with its confidential, natural tone and indifference to plot, can mask us and distract us.

I think, and now I speak as a reader, that the reader must have a sense of the writer there, that dialogue is implicit in art. Even Barthes, having dismissed him, later goes on to admit that in the text we "desire the author; [we] need his figure . . . as he needs [ours]." Just as every writer has an invisible, minatory reader dimly in mind, who says things like "she would never do that," or even, "don't put in so much description, can't you get along with the story faster?" the reader, for his part, has an invisible but tangible writer in mind to whom he says "how true" or "but if." Where there is no author, as in the case of oral literature or anonymous works, we tend either to invent him (never her, e.g., "Homer") or attribute the work to someone who does or did exist. Shakespeare is almost the oddest case, an author of such genius that he cannot have existed—I speak of the attempts to question his identity or ascribe his works to others. The easy appeal of the too autobiographical first-person narrative, however, can impede dialogue because one cannot challenge narrative elements compelled less by art than by circumstance.

I think a reader sees a writer as vividly as in a painting and we modify our image of him as a part of reading. We might see D. H. Lawrence wearing a lascivious smile until we realize he is kind of a prude whose inclusion of sexually explicit passages is the reflex of his discomfort with the whole subject of sex. Now we put a scowl on his face, rather like the scowl on the face of Carlyle. Dickens is fat. My own image of Twain comes from my childhood game of Authors. However you get it, this image changes according to the information you have, inferred from the attitudes, subject matter, and even mistakes we find in a book, and also what you might know of the author's real life. Our ideas about the writer may have come from that curious genre the literary biography. Why actually would one want to read about Wallace Stevens or Henry Green—the lives of most writers aren't very interesting—except to influence and clarify our malleable and developing image of a writer whose works we cherish, very much as we update the picture we have of our friends. We miss the author photo on the jacket if it isn't there. I have to tell you that when those four thousand people lined up before Louis L'Amour, clutching worn, beloved copies of his books, he refused to sign the paperbacks, only the hardbacks, and I've always wondered if those rejected readers went on reading him with as much affection as before.

I am not saying that the reader thus imposes a responsibility on you the writer in your daily life, to be a moral force or public figure. It may be that he tries, but I'm not talking at all about the writer's material self, his personality in the world, his media side. Let us pass over that. Writers like celebrity as much as the next person, but it never seems to have helped anyone write. Lionizing is not just a malady of the modern world—people have always seized upon writers if they are glamorous. They rarely are. We have all seen those spreads in *People,* say, the homely, ordinary-looking writer in his study, usually with some touching affectation of dress, say cowboy boots or a big hat, by which he hopes to set himself apart. Byron, or Marlowe, or Hemingway had glamour, but it is not given to most writers, nor to most mortals in any profession, not even for fifteen minutes. And most of us manage to avoid feeling too much regret about that. I should acknowledge that Louis L'Amour did not disappoint in glamour; he was a white-haired old man like the figure of God, and wore a great array of turquoise jewelry and a fringed buckskin Jacket.

The you in your text is not the same as you the living person. I was recently in Saudi Arabia, where women, even western women, are obliged to wear a kind of black choir-robe, called the abbaya, and a black head covering which is pulled across the face, rendering you invisible, though you can see, rather imperfectly, through the semitransparent fabric. Once invisible, I found myself to change, my personality changed. If I am, as I imagine, usually, reserved and polite, I became assertive and frank as I try to be in print. As I stood with a group of men at the hotel elevator, and they piled in and allowed the doors to close behind them without me, from beneath my veil I heard my own voice loudly and rudely denounce them as a bunch of jerks. Incidentally I should say that I felt that the veil, though symbolically odious, has this same liberating function for women in Islamic societies, in that it gives them license to speak without gender, and this is why they put up with it. About gender, I myself think the writer's persona has no particular sex in the text. The disadvantages of being a writer who is a woman are all external—the ghettoization of women's (and black, and gay) writing, the fact that men have to learn that they can read writing by women, something they often resist, the suspicion of female idiom—I mean the idiom of *Moby Dick* preferred to that of *Wuthering Heights,* two stories which greatly resemble each other; the unexamined assumption by critics that the great American novel will be written by a man—something which seems only half likely. I'm not sure the sex of the writer makes much difference to women readers because we are trained to read work by both sexes. I know as a reader I feel closer to Hemingway, a hunting, fishing sort of person from my part of Illinois and a fellow expatriate, than to English punk woman Angela Carter, or even, say, an American woman writing about an exotic New York world of shrinks and angst far from my experience.

The situation of a writer is like being veiled in Riyadh, invisible and explicit. As individuals we forget things, fail to think of the snappy response at a dinner table, are struck dumb at times we should strike back and so on. People like to meet writers, but they are mostly disappointed meeting them. It usually turns out that the drab mortal who gratefully accepts the glass of white wine after the reading or who plainly longs to get back to the hotel, is less than the passionate and clever personages on her pages. Our books are ourselves veiled, assertive and bold.

Another aside: when you begin as a writer you have to learn to accept that many strangers are going to have an opinion of your personal defects and hangups, and that your families—this is almost the hardest thing for writers to get used to when they begin—will come to know that you know things about sex or swear-words they didn't know you knew. It is amazing but true that the families of writers often don't read them, finding it too odd or painful. And it's a curious feature of writer photographs, that in an article containing a review of your book, and a photo, if both are bad, it is the photo you are apt to mind most. There is room for feeling that a reviewer has misunderstood your work, it is a complex work, after all, capable of many interpretations, but there is no mistaking your face.

But just as there is usually a gap between the real and the ideal character of the writer, there is also always a gap between what the writer means to do and how his book turns out. The gap is large. Critics tend to forget this. Any literary work is testimony to our failed intentions. Your book never turns out to be as good as you had hoped, back when you were thinking it up, before you went and spoiled it by writing it down. We know, if critics don't, that our novel is witness to our lapses of attention, hangovers, diminished stamina, boredom, unwise enthusiasms and so on. But the reader reads, I believe, with the implicit assumption that the writer is an authority, worthy of standing behind the work, who somehow gives permission to read and enjoy, perhaps by his very reliability assuaging the guilt we may feel at indulging in fantasy and giving ourselves up to stories—the reasons people are apt to say that fiction is less worthwhile than non-fiction. If, as Simon O. Lesser puts it, in his endearing and still illuminating *Fiction and the Unconscious,* "fiction . . . provides us with images of our emotional problems expressed in an idiom of characters and events," we need to have confidence in the person who provides these images, just as we need to have confidence in our grocer.

All this is to say that the writer's character comes under a certain scrutiny as it is revealed in all the main narrative elements of a fiction—style, subject, plot. In a poem too, no doubt. But where do we actually find the writer? How are we aware of his or her distinctive timbre, as Willa Cather called it, in narratives other than first-person ones? Style, to begin with. Take this sentence: "I won't even compare you with something I have a sort of dim stupid sense you might be and are not—for I don't in the least know that you might be it, after all, or whether, if you were, you wouldn't cease to be that something you are that makes me write to you thus." (Henry James to William Dean Howells) We recognize this writer by his style and only eventually by his rather censorious morality masked with urbanity. "Into the dark, smoky restaurant, smelling of the rich raw foods on the buffet, slid Nicole's sky-blue suit like a segment of the weather outside." That is the exuberant Fitzgerald. The narrator in *Howards End* strikes us as being like E. M. Forster, a Cambridge don, when he writes:

> The boy, Leonard Bast, stood at the extreme verge of gentility. . . . He knew that he was poor, and would admit it; he could have died sooner than confess any inferiority to the rich. This may be splendid of him. But he was inferior to most rich people, there is not the least doubt of it. He was not as courteous as the average rich man, nor as intelligent, nor as healthy, nor as lovable.

Here the writer and the narrator are surely one, E. M. Forster snobbish, judgmental, and perceptive. When we respond to the artfulness or peculiarity of a phrase, I think we always attribute it not to the narrator but directly to the writer, mentally congratulating him or complaining. Beside style, choice of subject is obviously an authorial Rorschach too—your preoccupations are formed for whatever reason, and you are the product of your experiences, though of course you can transcend them. We all tend to repeat ourselves or be known by our obsessions.

Saul Bellow dismissed plot as "unfit," seconding Gertrude Stein's opinion that it's rather low to just read novels for what happens next—Bellow mentions *Remembrance of Things Past* and *Ulysses* as novels we don't read for the story. I think we do, in fact. I've given some thought to the role of plot in writing fiction, and think it is honorable and essential, a vital activity of the novelist that has been unfairly stigmatized, with all the negative connotations of the word "plot," "plotting" meaning treachery and manipulation. About plot, the dismissive attitude grew up perhaps because, after Freud, we tried to think about all action as stemming from character, and character in turn as stemming from accidents of nurture, all determined beforehand by the logic or illogic of psychology, so that therefore "plot" with its adventitious surprises came to be seen as a mean property of the lower orders of popular literature, manipulative, not serious, and not art. By plot I mean the telling way a writer rearranges the elements of his or her experience and observation into a meaningful and absorbing ideal form that concentrates life in a way that meandering reality cannot. Bellow meant "narcotic or brain-washing entertainments, at worst breeding strange vices," which seems a little severe.

Anyone who has written a novel knows that the writer spends quite a bit of time plotting—deciding, say, whether Jeffrey will go to Detroit before or after meeting Nora, a decision with massive implications when it comes to who knows what is in the bank vault, matters wrestled with by the artist which boil down on the page to writing the one word, Thursday, instead of Sunday, and reversing two chapters—in other words in reflecting upon and manipulating a dynamic that is never expressed in words on the page, exactly, but which generates in the reader's understanding, like the synapse of a sparkplug across the empty space between the points, all the energy of the narrative. Plotting and, more peculiarly, errors in plotting (too obvious coincidence or banal ending) are one of the invisible aspects of narration for which the writer takes responsibility and gets blamed or gets the credit. It is in his plot arrangement that the novelist is most herself, himself, where his attitudes toward life and chance, his optimism, pessimism, his merriness or mysticism speak most directly to the reader. With plot, style, subject, an author communicates the preoccupations and habits of her mind. But style, plot, and authority are the very elements that fiction has somehow been losing.

Sometimes the writer fails to communicate. To illustrate communication let's say I, the reader, am an animal lover, fond of cats and dogs. In *Wuthering Heights,* a character drowns some puppies; this may anger me with him, but I also know that Bronte is using this example of brutality to tell us something about his spiritual state. I infer that she knows how this scene will affect me because she and I are operating in the same universe of dog lovers, and thus I can have some confidence in the symbolic meanings that underlie other things that will happen in the novel.

But sometimes we don't know what a writer means. In Christina Stead's autobiographical *I'm Dying Laughing* there is a scene where the heroine and person we judge to be nearest to the writer, is debating the course of her life. This is the scene where the title line is uttered. "I'm dying laughing," so we know it is an important, portentous moment of political and artistic truth. In the course of it, Emily finds a stray cat in her Hollywood kitchen. "The kitchen was in order and faultlessly clean; but an unwashed baking dish had been put on the floor for the cat to lick at. Emily shouted, with an ugly expression, 'Who did that?'"

"She took the cat by the scruff of the neck and hauled it to the door. It was a bluish, short-haired animal with a white hourglass on the belly. It had just had kittens. It was almost starved to death. She threw it out on the hillside which rose behind the house." This passage tells us something about Emily—but what? And is it what Stead intends? We animal lovers might think Emily must be a cruel, selfish person and that Stead means us to think so, but here too are honorific images of cleanliness and aprons. One fears that Stead agrees with Emily that stray cats are a nuisance, but we are not sure. I'm afraid I think of Christina Stead as cruel to cats.

Usually, the writer, careful not to be mistaken for one of his immoral, or criminal, or foolish creations, will insert sly reservations to indicate his own disapproval of someone who mistreats cats. Parenthetically it is worth mentioning that an author will usually be confounded with his creations, and this is especially true for women writers, who are freely assumed to have the morals or tragic lives of their heroines. It is not at all unusual to receive commiserating letters, or else reproaches. How brave of you to put up with living in that slum. How sad that you lost your mother in that theater fire. I think women are unconsciously assumed to have deficient powers of invention—so what you write must be true. Paradoxically women have also always been thought, by men at least, to be great liars.

But the point is, there's a reader-writer dialogue, and if you are the writer, the reader is interested in you. We might finally ask, what are the qualities readers hope to find in you, do find in the greatest writers over the heads of their creations? What do they want from a writer? Obviously it is not personal goodness, since we tend to like writers *in propria persona* to be a little bad, like Byron, or ill-fated in some way, flawed, drunk like Hammett or Malcolm Lowry—we want them to be a little like ourselves. But not too much. Of course, just as our face is not entirely within our control, the authorial self we reveal in our books is not entirely within our control, is so much oneself that there isn't much one can do about him or her except by trying to be better or taking Prozac or undergoing religious conversion—there are only a few ways people do change. The reader can see things in us we cannot see ourselves. It's not as simple as looking to the writer for moral guidance, even though he punishes the wicked and rewards the good, or, according to the conventional ironies of our own day, punishes the good and rewards the wicked. What we want is more a sense of observantness and ambivalence, a person of two minds about the impulses of the human heart, questioning of the criteria of conventional morality. Ambivalence—the side of Shakespeare that admired Macbeth's ambition and overreaching, the thing that produced Mozart's fondness for Don Giovanni. If it is true that the greatest fiction is pervaded by a sense of the opposite (it is only inferior fiction that tends to state things too boldly in black and white, as Bellow complained), this sense is likely to issue from the writer's simultaneous grasp, as Fitzgerald put it, of two contradictory ideas. Grasp is not a bad word. We want the sense that the writer has grasped things in all their complexity and has found for them a design whose formal properties and very words release and stir us. The author can't necessarily be "good," as in faithful, sober, generous, moral in conventional terms or saintly around the house; but what he must be is a complex receptacle of virtues all the same, if forgiving and understanding are virtues. He must know something beyond himself. It's this we tend to miss in recent fiction, I think.

I've been living in France. Sometimes it's good to be away because when you re-enter you have a day or two of revealing culture shock before everything begins to seem normal to you—will be struck by how fat Americans are, how all the formerly vigorous TV journalists now seem to be wearing weird toupees, and how the serious fiction now is terse, grisly and self-pitying at the same time, mostly concerning abuse of the author's self or the indignities endured by his/her grandparents. Really, since we are here, most of our grandparents are by definition fortunate. Don't we have something else to talk about? Conceptions of virtue, for example, or the operation of our social institutions? When you come back, you hear everyone saying that our culture is finished, is unlivable, ungovernable, getting dumber. Couldn't we talk about that? I consider myself a novelist of manners, a subgenre so distant from the mainstream that this isn't usually even understood. I guess I am a novelist of manners because I came from a small Midwestern town where one could still follow the action of society on the individual. But this is old-fashioned. The great nineteenth-century novelists had one subject, which could loosely be called "how to live." We don't have that because, hey, we can't tell anyone else how to live. Victorian writers wrote about their own experience, but did so in order to put a stitch in the great tapestry of literature which tries to present the human condition. Writers today want not just money but sympathy too. I guess I think that personal witness still has value—is finally all a writer can do—but the work of a career in writing should be to refine our skills as witness and use the personal to transcend the personal.

A friend of mine showed me the manuscript of his novel. "At last

I've come to understand my mother," he said. Writing a novel may indeed help you to understand your mother. Writing a novel is certainly a way of avoiding the psychoanalyst. Not even Freud wanted to tamper with the artist's mysterious powers. Roland Barthes, who seemed to have an apt observation about everything, said the motto of the writer ought to be "mad I cannot be, sane I do not deign to be, neurotic I may be," neurosis perhaps too severe a name for a powerful impulse to rearrange a less than ideal world into a better form, if only by revealing its flaws. But is American literature to become the sum of autobiographies vying for attention, like siblings on a stage? Maybe it is part of our collective loss of confidence in ourselves, an American as well as a writerly problem, that we have no larger subjects at the moment, but I think we have come to believe we have no stories to tell except, diffidently or defiantly, our own stories. And I think those are no longer enough, because we have arrived at a point in America where we can no longer understand each others' stories, or don't want to, are too ravished by the vibrancy of our own suffering, enamored of our too-facile way of appealing in all our frailty to the sympathy of others. Pain is the fashionable word. One trouble is that voices in pain tend to sound all alike, loud cries of pain drowning out thought and language. Do we have a duty to something larger? Duty is a word we tend to avoid; I know people always deplore the times they live in, but the lack of impulse to think about the inner life of others says something bad about us, and I think it is also significant, and bad, that in America, just now, no writer is considered dangerous to the state.

Fear of Happiness

Louise Glück

Among the distinguishing characteristics of mythic or totemic stories, let me call two of the most obvious to your attention: first, by definition, they stay in the mind—durability distinguishes the archetypal from the anecdotal. Second, more peculiarly, they mutate, or our perceptions of their fundamental truths change. Perhaps "mutate" is inaccurate; better to say that what magnetizes attention shifts. A story with staying power will offer a variety of possible centers of focus (though these may be perceived sequentially rather than simultaneously). Stories of this type, whatever their scale (and they may, superficially, resemble the anecdote), possess a certain interior spaciousness within clear outlines, so that they seem, on reflection, at once copious and eternally unresolved. In simpler terms, every time I see *Children of Paradise* it has a different hero. And every time I read *Wuthering Heights,* I feel a different moral or emotional imperative. When I was sixteen: value passion. Meaning sacrifice anything to it. When I was twenty-five: be wary of passion's tendency to screen narcissism. And so on.

All this holds true, as well, in the realm of the personal. We have, each of us, certain charged stories or referents, the sorts of stories we tell those people we wish to befriend, so that they will see what has formed us. What is odd is that, over time, the same story can be used to make different points, though we may continue to befriend the same sorts of attractive strangers.

When I was in my early twenties and beginning, finally, to master in psychoanalysis the range of symptoms I had been controlled by, when I was able to perform dazzling acts like eating in the presence of other human beings; when I no longer needed to do the same tasks daily in the same order; when I was no longer wholly withdrawn (which is the common legacy of shame), I found myself suddenly terrified. A vision of desolate normalcy presented itself. I was terrified, specifically, that

---

The Hopwood Lecture, 1996

normalcy—whatever I meant by that—would somehow eradicate the need for or capacity for what even then I ceremoniously called my work. For five years I had been struggling desperately to become whole and sane in order to rejoin a world made, as I saw it, entirely of the whole and the sane, a world free of the humiliating loneliness and fear that constituted my reality. And I remember very clearly my panic and the terms in which I accused my analyst, who had conspired in all this: he was going to make me so happy I wouldn't write. I also remember his response. He looked at me directly, an event in itself rare (and possibly the underlying reason I remember this exchange). His response was memorably succinct. The world, he told me, will provide you sorrow enough.

For the egotist, a revolutionary concept. What interested me in this story initially was the analyst's unprecedented directness together with the sense that his personal history had, briefly, entered the room. Also the strange unease his response provoked. My confidence in him was, for complex reasons, shaken. He had no right to be so present in the room, to substitute for Delphic silence and sly direction a remark so tainted by the personal. Also, I thought he was wrong. That is, I thought the world couldn't possibly provide as much anguish as I needed. If he was wrong, I had duped him; if I had duped him, he was no longer reliable. Did he really know how wily I was, how inherently powerful (despite the present restrictions of performance); did he really think the world was any match for such force? *I* generated my sorrow; nothing and no one could be trusted to meet my fierce and specific standard. Later, his remark took on an aspect of prophecy, which always has about it something of the echo—in this case, what was echoed was my own early perception of the world in exactly the aspect my analyst noted. Growing up, I had transformed myself into the agent of the inescapable; I couldn't bear chance, as a principle; I saw the world as whimsical and lethal, a machine for doing harm. And took over its work, to avoid being its victim.

In fact, it wasn't until very recently that I began to read this exchange from another angle, to examine a certain underlying assumption. Specifically, why was I so sure unhappiness was essential to the making of art? Or, more precisely, what attributes of what I imagined happiness to be did I believe subverted creation? Plainly, I ascribed to happiness some opacity or chronic unresponsiveness; accurately enough, I saw responsiveness as essential to the creative act, but my definition seemed to limit it to a particular type. I saw responsiveness, it appears, as resulting from a keenly felt abrasiveness between the self and the world, as though that boundary could be perceived only in the most dramatic and negative terms. What is emphasized in such definitions is the self, not as a secure pole or referent, but as a fundamental dimness clarified by oppositions. Its very haziness gives rise to its avidity; it strives constantly to define itself (as more clearly realized selves do not), and it is able to define itself only relative to what it is not.

In the period of which I've been speaking, whatever my surprise at my analyst's observation, I had a somewhat diminished stake in maintaining the presumably fecund misery from which, in my view, he insisted on rescuing me. Luckily, or so I presently believe, I was protected from my asserted wish to shore up suffering, to stabilize it, by the intensity of my suffering at that time. I had, too, this recent memory: I began analysis imperiled not by happiness but by despair; in the years that was most acute, I was wholly silent, on the page and in the world.

Set aside, for the moment, natural speculation regarding the talent of the artist, of the restless, demanding, insatiable soul, for actually attracting and sustaining serenity. Assume, for the moment, that some parenthesis of well-being does, from time to time, open, even in the lives of people of this type. Think, for now, only of the meticulous resistance to that state, which perhaps some of you have felt already. As in tlie moment when love ceases to be narrative, ceases to be dramatic capitulation, and the single next thing appears to be sterility, a vista of suburbs. As though the suburbs, as though the mutations of love in time, could only be sterile.

Curiously, once the question is posed, once the whole issue of the relation of unhappiness to the making of art comes under scrutiny, the sources of this connection grow clear. They derive, I think, from the original set of impulses and rewards that draw individual minds to this vocation. Most artists, most writers certainly, are drawn to the creative act by its capacity to promote catharsis and, through catharsis, affirm a faltering sense of power. Pre-existing anguish, in being given form, is externalized; in being externalized, it is transformed. Transformed, as opposed to neutralized; it gives rise to its extreme opposite. What results, for the artist or nascent artist, is euphoria. Not only are anxiety and tension temporarily relieved—something comes into being to which the self bonds with a kind of desperate ardor. Unfortunately, the learned dynamics of catharsis, the conversion via writing of despair to elation, will not sustain a creative gift any more than the animating rages of youth can be mechanically prolonged. Equally unfortunately, the more efficiently catharsis reins in suffering, and the headier the sense of elation that results from the making of a work of art, the greater the self's investment in art. In art, obviously, but also in the increasingly ritualized process leading to art. And ultimately an odd shadow of dependency or addiction creeps in. Suffering gradually becomes the presumed first condition of elation or triumph; the more efficiently catharsis works, the more likely it is that an artist is being created, a person, that is, whose sense of power and worth depends primarily on these surrogates, these objects it has created.

This dependency is my subject, and, beyond it, a certain practical speculation as to the usefulness, to an artist, of happiness, in whatever form it may happen to present itself. By which term I mean not euphoria (which is in any case familiar to people of this type, a state of grace like falling in love, and, like falling in love, an intoxication)—not euphoria, but that strange country I glimpsed in my analyst's office, happiness defined as well-being.

The artist, that person whose sense of self absolutely depends on continued creation, begins to connect his survival as a powerful, or in any case, viable being to despair; despair, however damaging, however threatening, however eroding of the physical self, cannot damage what is perceived as being truly essential: the ability to make art. Quite the reverse: this it preserves and sustains. The real threat, according to this reasoning, is happiness which, by removing active unrest, sabotages creative life, which proceeds from an accumulated misery that demands cathartic release. The dependency on dissatisfaction, the courting of it by the artist—this is less a Faustian compact than a destructive, or at least limiting, hope. Destructive not in the obvious sense, in that it places at risk or undermines the whole world of relationship, or physical soundness, or social function, but destructive in exactly those terms by which the self experiences its deepest sense of authentic being: what is threatened with destruction in this system is the artist, who was born, long before, not only of will but of its hopeless and powerless opposite, out of lack of control.

At the heart of this dilemma, the tacit rejection of happiness, is the problem of control, which is, first, the problem of vulnerability. It is the latter that attaches to happiness, to any form of *having*. Like material wealth, emotional or spiritual wealth stands to be lost: better the security of having nothing than the anxiety of well-being, which can only diminish. Moreover, the willed renunciation of well-being acts as a kind of protection: no one, the artist reasons, gets everything. So renunciation of what others hold most dear shores up, in the artist, what *he* holds most dear, his talent. And whatever its size, it is likely to be perceived, with some regularity, as precarious. The unfamiliar unnerves; in this system, misery and despair tend to produce an odd repose—they are at least known; they generate no obsession with subtraction, since they are that state to which subtraction ultimately descends. When nothing exists that can be taken away, a secret power asserts itself, a sense of control that well-being systematically threatens or erodes.

An early form of the pattern will seem, I believe, familiar. Put simply: once the addiction is established, despair becomes safety, and the artist begins to attempt to control or limit the ways in which he is influenced, trying to replicate indefinitely those circumstances or states of mind believed to be favorable to the making of art. This puts the matter, perhaps, too optimistically, makes choice seem to exist. Whereas the artist is, more likely, a being who has found a marginally viable existence which he goes on to frantically defend. His frenzy is natural, a function of the conviction that the alternative to present modes is not different modes but nothing, the abyss. This cleaving to pattern can coexist with apparently expansive or experimental behaviors, since what is being cleaved to is an edge, that is, precariousness. Only those experiences or behaviors characteristic of what we can loosely call normalcy or serenity are ruled out. And this comes to be a ruling against the unknown in its most radical form, a ruling made, oddly enough, in the name of risk.

Over time, the true danger, the true sabotaging routine domestic space becomes that edge to which panic roots the creative being. The words by which this edge is described affirm its glamorous shakiness; in fact, it has become wholly conservative space. I have seen this particular timidity in my own nature; I have watched it and heard it in my students. It fuels those questions about the future in which multiple desires or leanings figure: is it dangerous for a writer to be an academic? Will medicine (or law or business) destroy my gift? And, particularly among women, should I marry? Should I have children? And although no one can guarantee that the married doctor with children will also write enduring poetry, or that the passionate adolescent who finally permits himself maturity and pleasure will evolve into a deeper thinker, the person who, through cautious clinging to the known, the ostensibly safe, arrests or constrains his native fascination with medicine or desire for family is diminishing the possibility of his making original art. Meaning art unique to a specific and profoundly lived experience. Only such art attains the force and durability of paradigm. Whereas the "paradigmatic" artistic life, the edge I have been describing, when clung to through will, yields up an art hardly deserving of that name, an art too predictable in its judgments and, finally, too superficial to attract attention over time.

Behind the choice of despair (as opposed to the accident of despair, as opposed, also, to the tragic vision, which is another matter)—behind this choice is the unarticulated assumption that the life most conducive to art is entirely empty of anything interesting enough to distract from writing or satisfying enough to replace the need to write. But the earlier, the formative despair, the galvanizing memorable despair of adolescence, is not replicated through willful perpetuations and imitations. And the sadder form of these questions about the future is not question but statement, the asserted decision to turn from a natural bent lest the gift be damaged.

This is the mathematics of insurance (which insulates against the more painful perception of injustice). The need to write, or make art, gives rise to the wish to keep alive and affirm *only* the creative being and suppress or constrain all satellite selves. And as the only emotion held to be entirely safe to that being is unhappiness, the only congenial conditions turmoil and retreat, the only activity held to be free of environmental contamination and harmful distraction is the reading of great literature.

But once literature is sought for these reasons, it changes. Whatever it was once, infinite and necessary air, it now becomes restriction, less that air than the conditioned air of a sealed room. That is, it is being valued for what it is not; it is being used to screen out impurity. Or, to use another figure, it becomes something like steamed vegetables, safe because they contain nothing known to cause harm. To read for these reasons, to read to stay safe, is to undermine the essential capacity and service of literature. Those gifts become accessible again when less elevated pleasures are accommodated. Pleasures like cooking and bad movies, pleasures like the indefensible television's. I believe these pleasures also nourish though in mysterious ways: they relax the soul. They are the little worlds in which the spirit is not tested. The difficulty is that the artist cannot take pride in what they nourish because pride, in him, is so utterly connected to the creative act, and because his imagination concerning that act is limited by fear to a kind of magical system, rife with taboos and forbidden gestures. And, to people of this type, what is not a source of pride is, de facto, a source of shame.

Let me urge now the utility of happiness. First: understand that happiness or well-being does not automatically produce a poetry or prose that sounds these same sanguine notes. What is far more likely, certainly in the artist whose vision is tragic, is that some measure of well-being strengthens him sufficiently to enable the deepest excavations. The spirit, fortified, can afford to go more profoundly, more resourcefully, into its materials, being less imperiled. But principally I wish to argue for well-being as a means of increasing openness to diversity and, by extension, a means by which the artist increases his range or, possibly, locates a fundamental subject. Dependency on despair acts to limit the subjects with which the mind contends or engages to those subjects available at the time the rituals of catharsis were discovered. In my own experience, periods of despair resemble one another, even to the sense that each seems, at the moment and despite its antecedents, the true platonic desolation, the terminus, the authentic nadir. Whereas happiness surprises in both its advent and its causes: it releases information. What unhappiness tends to perpetuate is an isolating and, usually, limiting fixation on the self: except in the very rarest cases, this is bound to be an aesthetic limitation. Whereas well-being, in paying homage to its sources and causes, seeks out the world, a place likely to be more varied than the self, particularly than the artist self, so long protected from dubious influence. In periods of well-being, the world of external object and event enters perception. Focus moves outward as well as inward.

I believe my analyst was correct in his remark. The world, whether zealously monitored or allowed a looser hand—the world will indeed provide sorrow enough. The intensity and frequency and type of that sorrow depend to a painful extent on luck, which is called luck because it cannot be controlled or lured or annexed. We can't do anything about whatever luck decides to do with us. We can, however, refuse the narrowness of that determined unhappiness the will insists on. Occasionally something will give pleasure, will actually charm or divert or entertain, will, to use that terrifying word, disarm. Insofar as our fearful, compulsive, rigid natures allow, I think we should welcome what follows, since for natures of this kind, there is no embrace until one has been disarmed.

Two Journeys

Philip Levine

Is what follows a fiction by Balzac? It would seem unlikely, for there is no one standing out in the dark on a rain-swept night as a carriage pulled by six gray horses splashes down the Boulevard Raspail on the way to the apartment of that singularly beautiful woman, Madame La Pointe, although it does involve a beautiful and singularly gifted woman. Is it a fiction at all? That is a harder question to deal with. If Norman Mailer had written it and its central character were a novelist living in Brooklyn, the author of an astonishingly successful first book called *The Naked and the Dead,* a man deeply immersed in an ongoing depiction of the CIA, he would describe it as a fiction, and he would most likely name the central character Norman Mailer. One of my central characters is named Philip Levine, he is a poet from Detroit, he lives mainly in Fresno, California, where he has an awful job teaching too many courses in freshman comp at the local college, and on this particular summer day he is traveling with two fellow poets by train to give a reading almost no one will attend. It is twenty years ago, he is in his fiftieth year, as I was then, and though I cannot call it a fiction, I will begin now to fictionalize this tale.

I will say the local railway has a reputation for first-rate service, they are never more than a few minutes late even in the worst weather, and on this day the weather is a delight: blue sky with a few puffy clouds overhead as the poets head for the provincial town where their reading, though almost entirely unadvertised, will become the event of that summer's cultural history, a history that will never be written except for the present effort, which since it may be a fiction may not be a history at all. Shall I say that the events I am about to recount are as true as an old man's memory allows them to be? No, that would not be true, for I am about to give the other two poets fictional names and disguise them so as to protect them. Protect them from what or from whom? Neither

The Hopwood Lecture, 1997

does anything to be ashamed of; indeed both behave with marvelous integrity. I will protect them from me, that untrustworthy poet who might alchemize them into former production line workers or assemblers of universal joints and thus ennoble them to a degree that would appall both them and you. I will remain Philip Levine, 49 years old, six months from my seventh book of poetry, *The Names of the Lost,* and my first terrible reviews by that great friend to poetry, the *New York Times.* The other two poets I will give fictional names. The man, just approaching middle age, is slender, taller than I, and though still in his thirties his hair is beginning to go gray, but he is far more youthful and youthful-looking than I, and unlike me he dresses with good taste. His name, Gabriel Sienna. The woman is even younger; she is fair-haired, delicately constructed, and in the soft light falling into our car very beautiful—I shall call her Elaine Langer—though she cannot be much over thirty her poems have already begun to attract enormous attention.

I am pleased to be here with these two who I am beginning to like far more than I expected. Sienna, I had heard was something of a dandy and a political conservative, but for the past several days I have observed him treating working class people—waiters, maids, cab drivers, cops, train conductors—with a grace and regard that I immediately recognized was part of his democratic nature. Elaine had been a mystery to me. I had met her only twice before when we'd read together in New York City and Iowa, and both times she had insisted on referring to me as the star. To me a star was Marlon Brando or Willie Mays, so I had assumed—incorrectly—that she was either ditzy or sucking up to me in the hopes I might advance her career, but it was now clear to me that she was not so stupid as to think I was endowed to advance anyone's career, even my own. In the few days we'd been traveling together it had become clear that she was neither ditzy nor a careerist: she was simply a shy woman. That she had not the least interest in me or Sienna as sexual or romantic beings was clear from the moment we'd assembled in the capital, for she was mad about a very handsome, stylishly dressed young man who sat sleeping across the aisle from the three of us, perhaps exhausted by the previous night.

To our mutual delight Sienna and I had discovered that before this trip we had both been rereading *The Prelude* by Wordsworth and finding it both awesome and inspiring. For me this was largely unexpected, for I had not read the entire poem since my undergraduate days when my professor had forced a class of a dozen students to race through it in less than a week and to keep our eyes open for the key passages which might indicate its deeper themes. Rereading the poem in my own sweet time I discovered the majesty of passage after passage, which reaffirmed my belief in this art I seemed to be giving my life to. Elaine broke in at one point to express her astonishment that two active poets would spend so much of their summers on so dated a text and would both feel the experience had fueled their own work. She was not in the least critical. To the contrary; she was utterly charmed and vowed that when these readings were over and she was home she would sit down with Wordsworth and Keats (who had been the topic of the previous day's train conversation) and discover for herself these treasures. Here the fiction or the history or the poem—for as Edwin Muir has reminded us, "the poet's first allegiance is to imaginative truth" and "if he is to serve mankind that is the only way he can do it"—grows crucial, for one of us, Sienna or I, asks where she had received her education in poetry. (For the purposes of this "history" I will invent a university and place it in Peoria, the University of Ambition, famous for its dedication to the arts, often referred to as "the Athens of Central Illinois.") Elaine answers, "U of A," and Sienna then inquires if she had not been obliged to read the great Romantics. At this point tears well up in her eyes, and it is clear that some memory just come upon her is devastatingly painful. The three of us are silent for several minutes.

Elaine wipes her eyes with the back of her hand; she does not cry. She begins a slow explanation: she had gone to the university with the express purpose of becoming a poet. She was some years older than the other entering students, having done "other things" after finishing high school, and one of the other things was to try to become a writer on her own, chiefly a writer of poetry. She knew no one in her New Jersey town who wrote poetry so she had to go it alone and discover what she could. In the local library and in New York City bookstores she happened upon three kindred spirits: Louise Bogan, James Wright, and Theodore Roethke, but she was sure there were many others and hence her enrollment at U of A. Her entrance scores were good enough to allow her into poetry writing and a "period course" in the Romantic poets, courses usually reserved for juniors and seniors. "So you've read Keats and Wordsworth," I say, "and you've been sitting here for two days listening to us mis-describe their great poems." Once again I had it wrong. While they were still on Blake and what her teacher termed "the Pre-Romantic poets," he had asked her to visit his office so that they might discuss her Blake paper. And then she laughs, her face full of lively animation as well as sorrow. They never got to her paper. Tweedy Professor X put down his unlighted pipe and launched into a spiel about the evils of nursing an unacted desire, both his and hers, for he was quite sure they felt *that way* about each other. The lust of the goat, he assured her, is the bounty of God and one law for the lion and ox is oppression (he didn't say which one he was); he placed a long-fingered hairless hand on her knee. "Long fingered and hairless," she repeats, "I will remember that hand for as long as I live." She felt the sweat leap from her pores, and for a moment she thought she would faint. "What did you do?" asks Sienna. "I just got out of there." She dropped the course.

Elaine goes on to explain that it was actually more serious than it sounded in the telling, for she began for the first time in her life to doubt the value of poetry, to doubt the whole enterprise. This of course was noticed by her poetry-writing instructor, a short, balding man much impressed with his own wit and vitality. He required the students to turn in poems written according to strict formal demands. He had lavishly praised her first two attempts, ten heroic couplets and a Petrarchan sonnet, which were followed by no villanelle, no pantoum, no narrative in blank verse. Professor Y, or Mac, as he insisted his students call him, asked Elaine to stay after class on their sixth meeting. When the other students had departed, he closed the classroom door, turned suddenly toward her, and literally shouted, "What the fuck is going on?" He began a long rap on the theme of her special gifts and his generosity in allowing her into the class in the first place. Before she could begin to describe her own problem, he launched into a tirade on the need for these beginners to follow the proper path, the path their elders had followed, the path that had produced such giants as Nemerov and Justice. She tried to assure him that her situation had nothing to do with the ongoing quarrels over formalism and free verse. "You have the talent to become a published poet within a year, and I have the clout to see you are published. I've done it for others." And then he began to rattle off the poets he'd "made," a word he used before each woman's name. His hands were short and plump; they looked as though they'd never picked up anything heavier than a check, and he placed one on her shoulder and began to slide it down toward her left breast when she rose and called him a "fat pig." She dropped out of the university that afternoon. "I'd had such hopes for the place," she says and goes on to describe her bus ride to Chicago, her confusing hours there, wondering if she'd done the right thing, and then the even longer lonely trip back to New Jersey. She spent the year as an office worker for a textbook publisher in New York City commuting from her parents' place.

"When did you get back to poetry?" Sienna asks. Within a month or so she realized she could not let herself be scarred by those two creeps; poetry was something she had to write, if only for herself. "It's a long story," she says, "but I had the good fortune to discover through a course at the 92nd Street Y a true mentor, also a man, but one who cared about me as a person as well as my work." Her lover, Daniel, has wakened across the aisle and is stretching himself. The train is drawing through the green suburbs of our destination; we pass tennis courts, most of them in use, a small white church, and then enter a darkened tunnel only to emerge into the terminal. We rise and that conversation comes to an end forever as Daniel struggles with the two huge suitcases loaded with the clothes, makeup, and tchotchkes of this small and determined woman.

Is the fiction you've just heard true? If Aristotle in the *Poetics* is right then it is truer than history, or to quote Edwin Muir again, it is "a symbolic stage on which the drama of human life can play itself out." Let me ask a more essential question: Is it of any use? Does it contain any nuggets of wisdom you can take with you on the long voyage toward a life in poetry, or if you would prefer, a life without poetry? Poetry itself we know is of use. How do we know such a thing, stated so finally by me as a fact that might sit beside such assertions as "all men are mortal," or "Michael Jordan wears Nikes"? I could answer as Keats would have, that I have tested it on my pulse and felt that pulse surge—a fact—and I knew that I was alive to a degree rare in my experience. Or as the contemporary poet Jane Cooper has written, "Poetry can be *useful* in providing us with a theater of total human responses." Cooper was in the process of defining the essential qualities of that very essential poet Muriel Rukeyser, who herself wrote in her book *The Life of Poetry,* "The making of a poem is the type of act which releases aggression. Since it is released appropriately, it is creation." If your nature is totally pragmatic you might demand to know if Marvell's "To His Coy Mistress," when heard by his beloved—for surely he intoned it to her in his rich baritone—caused her to become so much less coy that she rewarded his advances. A question I, of course, can't answer, but if Rukeyser is right, and I believe she is, it hardly matters, for the poem itself was an act of creation the rest of us have had joy in for centuries. If that other act of creation never transpired it may have mattered enormously to Andrew Marvell or perhaps not at all, for the poem may merely have been that symbolic stage Muir referred to.

Before I get back to the three poets in the provincial terminal waiting impatiently on wooden benches for the promised host to collect them—and Daniel, the lover, as well—and escort them to their hotel and there complete arrangements for that night's dinner and reading, I have something of a parable to share with you, one that deals with a life with poetry and a life without poetry. At age eighteen when I found the poetry in English of the last century and a half, Stephen Crane first, then Eliot, Auden, Spender, Wilfred Owen, Dylan Thomas, Yeats, Hardy, Stevens, Frost, Dickinson, Whitman, and finally Williams—I thought that without these words life would be a pale thing. I took Williams' famous words from "Asphodel, that Greeny Flower" very seriously and recited them to any innocent victim I could corner: "It is difficult / to get the news from poems / yet men die miserably every day / for lack / of what is found there." I took them to be about me and everyone else. To the credit of my patient students, many of whom went on to become poets while others opted for careers in law, medicine, wine making, journalism, organic farming, housewifery, and the military, when I stated and restated the absolute need of poetry in every life, no one laughed in my face or contradicted me.

Fortunately not everyone was so docile. At a poetry conference in Bisbee, Arizona, about a dozen years ago I went into my usual rant about the essential need for poetry in each life. No one in the audience blinked, but on the panel with me was that wonderful and very wise poet Robert Duncan who after hearing me out gently corrected me. He reminded me that we are not all alike: what turns some of us on bores others to death. He asked me if that indeed had not been my experience. Indeed it had been, I agreed, for at one time I had hoped that all productions of Wagner's operas be staged underwater, music which Mark Twain had once remarked was not as bad as it sounded. From then on I stopped badgering my students and friends and any other captive audiences. After listening to Duncan I came to believe that the teacher's function was not to force an art down the throats of his students but rather to help them find the art that thrilled their hearts.

Now for the parable. It bears some resemblance to the "history" or fiction of the three poets journeying to their reading, though there is one difference: it is composed of nothing but facts. It involves a poet journeying to a reading, a lone poet, one of the very same three, Levine, now a bit older, a bit tougher having survived a number of bad reviews, but not so tough that passing over the island of Manhattan where he will spend the weekend with his oldest son and then read for a small mob at the 92nd Street Y, he does not feel his secret heart swell with excitement, his pulse quicken, his breath surge as though he had just heard Galway Kinnell recite one of those magical passages from his great poem "The Avenue Bearing the Initial of Christ into the New World." So excited and perhaps foolish is he at that moment that he turns to the man seated next to him and says something profound, like "Isn't that amazing!" The man, a large, besuited fellow who has had his head stuck in a huge tome depicting some of the world's longest bridges, leans across Levine's lap to have a look and says, "My." A conversation ensues. The large man, it turns out, is headed for a conference on the uses of reinforced concrete. It will convene on Monday, at noon, in a large hotel that is part of the complex known as Dulles Airport. He had planned to change planes at La Guardia and fly directly to Dulles although this is Saturday afternoon, and he could just as easily spend two nights in New York City, for he is on an expense account. Levine calms the fellow's fears regarding the dangers of the city and assures him that if he stays away from the wrong neighborhoods he'll be just as safe as he'd be in Indianapolis where he works and lives. What could he do in New York? he wonders aloud. Almost anything, Levine replies. What are you interested in? No response. Does he like painting? The museums are among the best in the world. Painting is OK. How about theater or movies? A tepid response. Levine tries food, for every sort of ethnic food is available. Well, the fellow has to watch his weight, and he jabs a thick forefinger into his barely pouching waist and goes on to describe his incredible exercise regimen, though he avoids lifting weights for that can give you a false sense of power. Levine runs through dance, jazz, classical music, rock—which it turns out gives the fellow terrible headaches—; just walking the streets of what is probably the world's most energetic city can be a heady experience. The cement maven sits impassively. Levine offers to share a cab in from La Guardia and direct him to a nice hotel. After a long silence the poet says, I think it's probably best if you get to Dulles as quickly as possible.

So while I believe Duncan was right and since receiving his tactful remarks on my position regarding the situation of poetry in the world, I have never again browbeaten those who do not respond to it, write it, care if it exists at all. I have come to believe that something must be there to, as Jane Cooper so aptly put it, "provide us with a theater of total human responses." My seatmate on that flight into La Guardia is the perfect example of someone who lacks that theater, who seems to have no idea such a thing could exist. An educated man with a degree in engineering from Purdue, he must once or twice in his life have attended to a poem and barely noticed it as it flew by him on its way to glory. In my description of our conversation I left out one detail which occurred near its end: out of some growing distaste for the man as well as to determine the degree to which he had stopped being a total person, I added that Manhattan was full of the sexiest people I had ever seen, both men and women, and their styles of walking, talking, dress, made it clear just what treasures they possessed. For all he seemed to care I might have been describing varieties of apples. I went on: "You just see them on the streets in midtown or in the Village or Soho at all hours, bodies and faces the likes of which never filled the streets of the Midwest." His only response was, "I am married," which suggested to me not his moral rectitude—which may have been wonderfully intact—but his total lack of curiosity as to how people have been behaving for the last few thousand years.

I have at times considered a world totally without music and reacted with a horror so absolute that I immediately knew it was the art that fired my heart and blood like no other even though I have no talent for it. Thanks to the discoveries of Thomas Edison I have it even without New York City. Indeed in Fresno, where I have lived longer than anywhere else, I have it each morning when I waken to the mockingbirds doing their thing from on high in the Atlas cedar that grows in my front yard. But the art I have pursued for better or worse for over fifty years is poetry, and I have found it an enterprise worthy of a human life, and I haven't the least notion if anything I have written will in the hearts of others outlive me. Why, you might well ask, with that knowledge do I call it an enterprise worthy of a human life? Because I have been part of something far larger than myself: I have been part of the attempt to verbalize as precisely as possible what it has meant to live through the great depression, the horrors of World War II, the fiasco of anti-communism, the long, painful failed struggle for racial justice, and wind up in old age in a country gone to ruin through the greed of capitalism with a technology that can take us to the moon while our streets are stained by the lives of the poor and the homeless, the present world of Microsoft, unfettered pollution, the epidemic of murderous drugs, and the economic policies of Ronald Reagan, I have been part of the generation of Adrienne Rich, John Ashbery, Galway Kinnell, W. S. Merwin, Robert Creeley, Anthony Hecht, Denise Levertov, Etheridge Knight, Sylvia Plath, Allen Ginsberg, Gary Snyder: we have done our best to capture the century in verse. We have told America, and the rest of the world should it care to listen, what it's been like living through this age. We have been useful.

What has become of the three poets just arrived in the provincial town of X, justly famous for its great cathedral and its filthy brown river that drags slowly through the town? With Daniel the two men grow restless and begin to pace the gradually emptying train station while Elaine sits composedly staring off into the dusty building at nothing in particular. At last the emissary arrives with two taxis in tow, thank heavens for no single taxi can handle all the luggage Elaine has loaded upon the shoulders of her young lover as well as the three poets and their host. She, the emissary, is breathless and apologetic, and her apologies are quickly accepted, for the poets have learned they in fact have hotel rooms, plans for dinner, and an almost totally unannounced reading to give that night. The emissary, Catherine, who prefers to be called Cate, is both a younger and more attractive woman than those usually strapped with these functions; today she seems flustered and more than a little overwhelmed by her duties. Even before we reach the hotel we are warned that it is not top-notch as the local arts council is strapped for cash and also that due to a screwup by some hireling of the council the only advertising for the event consists of small posters placed "in just the important places" that very Saturday morning by Cate herself. "To have great poetry you need great audiences," Whitman had written, but I learned that night what I had suspected for years, that for once at least good father Walt was wrong.

After being deposited in our mediocre digs—one room with two single beds for Sienna and me, bath down the hall—we are free for some hours to walk the almost deserted town, inspect the massive local cathedral, and gaze longingly into the sluggish river a dozen local boys find suitable for a dip. We return to our room in time to shower and dress in the expected jackets and ties and meet with Elaine and Daniel in the tiny chairless lobby where a waiting Cate leads us a few blocks to a modest restaurant. The meal begins with something I still believe the waitress called sorghum soup and goes rapidly downhill from there. Cate keeps reminding us not to expect a crowd. No, there will be no books available for signing and sale; no one at the arts council knew how to go about obtaining them. When we arrive on foot at the community house at which we will read there is no audience at all besides the three young men arranging the lights and moving some of the furniture out of the way, for in fact we will be reading on the set of a Pinter play that will have its first performance the following week. We wait in silence until fifteen minutes past the assigned hour, but no one arrives. I ask the lighting technicians to stay and along with Cate to become our audience, and two agree to do so; the third has made arrangements for the evening but promises to return as soon as possible with his girlfriend. I read first after introducing myself, for Cate has confessed she has no idea who we are, what we have published if anything, and what our work might be about. I read as well as I have ever read, finding unusual strength in my voice and aiming my words toward my two fellow poets who have heard me for several nights in a row but never before seemed so alert to what I was reading. Elaine reads next after a short introduction by me; it is by far the best reading I have ever heard her give. She is usually nervous to the point of being almost inaudible, directing her attention not to her listeners but rather to an invisible audience riding ten or twelve feet above the actual one, but this night she looks directly into my eyes. I hear the fullness of her language, the delicacy of her rhythms, and the startling freshness of her tropes as I've never heard them before. She introduces the poems with only their titles and launches them into the utter silence of the room in a strong alto voice. Sienna comes next. He begins with no wisecracks or small talk but instead goes into a long and extraordinarily moving elegy to his father which he follows with three short lyric poems; this is far more daring and powerful work than he is known for. When he finishes, the six of us—Elaine, Daniel, Cate, the two technicians, and me—rise and applaud this stunning presentation and its creator. Before we can leave for drinks at the local watering hole "on the arts council," the third technician returns with his stunningly attractive friend in tow, and they are assured they have missed something astonishing. I suggest that each of us poets read one poem for these two, and to my surprise my fellow poets are equally enthusiastic. The magic is still there.

What startled me most and what I recall most clearly from that night was my sudden and overwhelming discovery of Elaine's poetry. For the first time I was truly getting it. Even in the theater of my mind, alone with the poem on the page, I had not attended to it with the intensity and passion it demanded. I had been reading her work as a series of bright moves, of smart decisions, I had been hearing harmonious phrases and lines moving gracefully from one to another, careful pacing and lovely ploys that brought the poems to a satisfying closure. That night I heard a unique human voice calling out from the deepest roots of its nature, calling out to be heard by what was deepest and most human in me. I was hearing poetry. We here in America have been practicing this art for hundreds of years almost without an audience for the single reason that we must in exactly the way a born dancer must respond to the music. That night Elaine had an audience—I know that as well as I know anything—and though it may have been only an audience of one, the act was complete, for one human being had reached across the immense gulf our education has taught us exists between each of us, had reached across that gulf through the magic of her language to remind me I was human.

Let me return to a question I asked earlier as a way of avoiding the question of the truth of this narrative: what use is this story? I think it contains two extraordinary truths about a life in poetry. The first is that we as poets (and no doubt also as people) need each other. As a boy first composing poetry at age thirteen I truly believed that some day I would be addressing the world. I was perfectly able to wait for that day, for the composing itself was such a delicious experience. Even at eighteen when I began my second career as a poet—my first was quite short, lasting less than three years and fortunately producing nothing that is extant—I thought that what I wrote in both prose and verse would have an enormous influence on the way my fellow citizens behaved toward themselves and each other. I had every reason to believe this, for the writers I was reading, especially the fiction writers (Dreiser, Dos Passos, Chekhov, Dostoyevsky, Balzac, Sherwood Anderson) were creating a me I had not known could exist. Within a year I would read Keats's letters, for me the most extraordinary document on what it means to be a poet, and again become someone else. Through the agency of his letter to his brother George on the world as the *Vale of Soul Making* I felt myself becoming a religious person. In the letter he asks George, and because the letter has been preserved those of us who will follow, what the use of a world like ours is and goes on to define that use. "There may be intelligences or sparks of divinity in millions," he writes, "but they are not Souls till they acquire identities, till each one is personally itself."

And how will this happen? "How, but by the medium of a world like this?" In order to clarify what he only dimly perceives he puts it "in the most homely form possible," and he goes on to tell George and us that the world is the horn book from which each intelligence learns to read, that is, to become what it is capable of becoming, a singular identity, a soul; without the education our experience of *this* world can give us we remain less than a soul, merely a potential. It is an extraordinary vision for a twenty-three year old man to coin to account for human suffering, which Keats knew full well as an apprentice surgeon working in a London hospital, but then Keats was one of the most extraordinary twenty-three year olds who ever lived. As the oldest of four siblings and with both parents long dead, Keats was deprived of what most of us take for granted, an adolescence. He had to become a man at a very early age; he had even to nurse his younger brother Tom through the final stages of TB to his death at eighteen. When he asked after the use of a world like ours he knew that world in its glory—his poems attest to that—and in its savagery. If Keats is right, the experience of this world can school each one of us into becoming a soul, and of course literature is part of the experience the world gives us. That night of the reading with an audience of no more than eight and no less than one, Elaine revived a human soul.

A genius such as Rimbaud or Dickinson or Blake can go it alone. There are those among us who are so gifted and so furiously and originally motivated that nothing can stop them from becoming poets except themselves. The rest of us need each other; we need to know this largely ignored art is still cherished and useful to others, and we need each other's counsel and encouragement to stay the course. (I suspect many of you have learned this or you wouldn't be at a place like this.) In my thirty-something years of teaching I've seen it over and over: one truly gifted and generous aspiring poet can excite an entire class and direct them to a poetry they did not know they possessed. In the fall of '61 a psychology major trying his hand at writing in my first poetry writing class rose in the back of the room and asked if he might offer a poem to the class. Thinking no harm could come from this I let him recite a piece he had not yet written down. It began thusly:

> If a broken-down roan in a fenced-in field had only two legs would it be
> a man?
> If a spotted dog wearing a napkin had one leg would it be a Republican?

If a man had common sense would the governor make him pick clover
for the next two thousand years?
In my last incarnation I looked for the perfect apple and so walked from
Albany to Sacramento
And chain-smoked the entire way.
My health is better for it so don't believe anything you read.

His name was Charles Moulton, and he was a genuine Fresno surrealist. To say the class never quite recovered from the experience is an understatement. Moulton had managed in a few minutes to fire the imaginations of twenty young and not so young poets who suddenly understood it was open house and that whatever the brain concocted was material for poetry. A few years later it was an entering freshman, Larry Levis, who wrote, "He numbed himself to photographs / of farmers swatting flames off their faces. / He lived at least / as well as a cold rat, // waiting for his number to come up." Yes, even the draft was material for poetry; Larry's classmates began to write utterly surprising poems that struggled with the agony and humor of coming to age or middle age in their brutal Central Valley towns. Two years later it was the lyricism of David St. John, also a freshman, that did the trick; later the sardonic anger of Sherley Williams and Gary Soto. It's amazing how far we can go with each other's help. The myth is that we must remain solitary and write out of the sources of our deepest woundings. Keats describes something totally different in another letter: "Whenever I find myself growing vaporish I rouse myself, wash and put on a clean shirt, brush my hair and clothes, tie my shoestrings neatly, and in fact adonize as I were going out—then all clean and comfortable I sit down to write. This I find the greatest relief." He prepares himself for company—for he loved the fellowship of men and women—and invites his muse in. The truth is we form a family with all the poets, living and dead, or we go nowhere.

The second truth I also learned from Elaine. The impulse, the drive, if you will, to write poetry is incredibly powerful. In spite of the worst efforts of two terrible men disguised as teachers, Elaine had only briefly been sidetracked. This young woman who at less than a hundred pounds and, as her early photographs attest, of a delicate beauty and, as I learned through the contact of some weeks, of a delicate emotional constitution contained an unkillable need to create true poetry, to build that "theater of total human responses." Each of us no doubt takes a differing and private route to this art (or in some cases away from it); those of us who need it, who see it as essential to our spiritual survival, will overcome the discouragements of an indifferent society and a corrupted literary world. We will do this simply because we have to. Why is this true? I believe the need to write poetry (and I assume prose fiction) is exactly like the need as Plato defines it to love, that is, to possess the halved soul's complement, to be whole. The sense of completeness that writing at our best gives is comparable to nothing else in my experience, but that is no doubt because I have no gift for music and can draw nothing that resembles anything. I don't see poetry as chief among the arts nor writing as chief among human vocations. Rather I see imaginative writing as one among many useful pursuits. Not long ago I heard the great tenor saxophonist Sonny Rollins say of his life in music, "Everybody has something to do in this world." Being able to play the music he loves he found a blessing. Being able to play it with Gillespie, Hawkins, Max Roach, Clifford Brown, and Coltrane he found a blessing far beyond his early hopes. From what I know of Rollins's life—and I know a lot—like Elaine nothing could stop him.

Of course when Rollins said each of us has something to do he meant something useful. In his case it was the making of music, and if you don't know why music is useful then there's nothing I can do to help you. And how useful is poetry? Let me go to one of the great writers of the century for a little help. In his essay "Why the Novel Matters," D. H. Lawrence writes, "As a man alive you may have a shot at your enemy. But as a ghastly simulacrum of life you may be firing bombs into men who are neither your friends or enemies, but things you are dead to: Which is criminal when the things happen to be alive." For Lawrence it is in the novel that we learn exactly what a man or woman alive is; by reading novels, "You can develop an instinct for life, if you will, instead of a theory of right and wrong, good and bad." The only three great novels Lawrence names in the essay are the Bible, Homer, and Shakespeare. He calls these "the supreme old novels," but as any reader knows, two are poetry and the other when it is at its most eloquent is also poetry. I don't have to lecture you on how completely contemporary life can deaden us to what is alive; you have all experienced it enough for me not to add an ounce to your burden. "The grass withereth, the flower fadeth, but the Word of the Lord shall stand forever," quotes Lawrence and goes on to claim, "That's the kind of stuff we've drugged ourselves with," for the truth is the grass comes back, the flower dies and gives birth to new buds, but "the Word of the Lord, being man-uttered and a mere vibration on the ether, becomes staler and staler, more and more boring till at last we turn a deaf ear and it ceases to exist." But truly imaginative writing can bring us back to the living presence of the grass, to the fields that feed us, to the cities we live in and the nature of the men and women among whom we live.

> Tenderly will I use you curling grass,
> It may be you transpire from the breasts of young men,
> It may be if I had known them I would have loved them,
> It may be you are from old people, or from offspring taken soon out of
> their mothers' laps,
> And here you are the mothers' laps.
>
> This grass is very dark to be from the white heads of old mothers,
> Darker than the colorless beards of old men,
> Dark to come from under the faint red roofs of mouths.

In fact the greatest of our poets can make us come alive to the world in all its richness to a degree we scarcely believe.

I confess I not only find poetry useful these days, I find it absolutely necessary. I am presently living in one of the most complex, turbulent, disturbing, unfathomable communities in the world: New York City. Even my twenty-six years in industrial Detroit failed to prepare me for this. But through the work of its poets—Whitman, Hart Crane, García Lorca, and Galway Kinnell—I have come not only to a degree of peace with all the tumult, I have also become so comprehending of its presence that at times I can see its ordinary diurnal street life as the arena of the sublime and the sacred:

> It is night, and raining. You look down
> Toward Houston in the rain, the living streets,
> Where instants of transcendence
> Drift in oceans of loathing and fear, like lanternfishes,
> Or phosphorous flashings in the sea, or the feverish light
> Skin is said to give off when the swimmer drowns at night.
>
> From the blind gut Pitt to the East River of Fishes
> The Avenue cobbles a swath through the discolored air,
> A roadway of refuse from the teeming shores and ghettos
> And the Caribbean Paradise, into the new ghetto and new paradise,

This God-forsaken Avenue bearing the initial of Christ
Through the haste and carelessness of the ages,
The sea standing in heaps, which keeps on collapsing,
Where the drowned suffer a C-change,
And remain the common poor.

Through the magic of language I live *my* daily life in Kinnell's City of God without God; that's how useful poetry can be.

What became of our three poets after their triumphant, scarcely attended reading? Their host, Cate, walked them to the local pub and there stood them to a drink on the arts council, and then they stood her to one on their meager stipends. The place was noisy with Saturday night celebrants, and so the poetry party came to a rather abrupt ending. The poets went off on foot to their shabby digs, at least two of them with the intention of sleeping. Elaine and Daniel may have had more serious work to do, for as Rilke reminds us those who make love do a very essential work. Exhausted, Sienna seemed to fall off before his head hit the pillow. Levine was too wired from the reading, and for more than an hour he sat on his bed writing in his journal that day's events without knowing that some day, perhaps today, he would find them useful. Finally he too grew weary and turned out the light and welcomed the darkness. Perhaps he slept. In any case all three poets rose the next morning from soiled beds to hurry off by cab to the station for still another voyage to still another tiny audience.

Let me close with a final cautionary tale. Some years ago I received a letter from a very dear man who also wrote poetry, had in fact published several books though none recently and altogether only a fragment of what he had written. To put it bluntly he was and is what the world might call "a failed poet" though he is a gifted writer. He is both unlucky and without any clout in what I will call the "church temporal" of poetry, that world of ass-kissing and favor-trading that brings so much useless work to acclaim. He had decided that even without a publisher he would put together his complete poems, and he did so under covers supplied by Kinko's. His letter was a response to this event, a dignified and touching letter which described his own emotions as he beheld this utterly unique volume. But he used one phrase that by now even he would regard as suspect; he wrote "now the granary is full." He sat for some weeks with this volume, finding its presence less and less satisfying and finally sent it off to a university press. Knowing the speed with which any press deals with poetry he grew restless and uncharacteristically crabby. He told me later he put his household into a state of anxiety it had not known for over thirty years, since the coming of children. The cure for these ills was his own and obvious: his need to be a useful person could not be quieted, so complete poems or not he went back to the day by day undramatic work of trying to make poems. The truth is, poets need poetry as much as poetry needs poets. This man knew, as all of us who write poetry know, that if the work is worthy eventually it *will* find its readers. It may take more years than we have, as it did in the case of Dickinson and Kit Smart, but our job is the work of creation and as such it never ends.

I'm frequently asked, especially by students, how I got into poetry and what kept me going. I always tell the truth: once when I was very young I heard a knock at the door; I was home alone and so I answered. There was a man in a bowler hat who asked if Philip Levine were home. "Yes," I said, "I am he." (Even then I was a stickler for grammar.) "My name is Tom Eliot," he said, "though you may know me as T. S. Eliot. I've come to tell you that American poetry needs you." What he was doing in a lower-middle class neighborhood in Detroit, a Jewish neighborhood no less, I wasn't sure, but as our only Poet Nobelist could I refuse him? You don't believe that and you shouldn't. No one asked me to try to become a poet; it's what I chose to do and it's what I choose to continue to do, and if it takes me nowhere I have no one to thank except myself.

Further Questions?

John Barth

Henry David Thoreau began one of his wonderful lectures by saying, "You have invited me; you have engaged to pay me; and I am determined that you shall *have* me, though I bore you beyond all precedent."

My resolve on this occasion is the same as Thoreau's. The better to implement it, I'm going to serve me up to you by asking myself and replying seriously to a number of altogether *un*exciting questions—the first of which, reasonably enough, is "Why bother to do that?"

Well: The fact is that like many another American writer in the second half of the twentieth century, I served my literary apprenticeship not in expatriate cafés or Depression-era boxcars or on the assorted killing fields of any of our several wars, but for better or worse in undergraduate college and then in graduate school—majoring in, of all things, *writing*. Ernest Hemingway would disapprove; likewise, no doubt, Charles Dickens, Honoré de Balzac, Mark Twain, and many another alumnus of the School of Hard Knocks. So did I, for that matter, now and then, for it was on such writers that I was raised. But except for a sculpting uncle of mine who attended the Maryland Institute's College of Art shortly before dying in the First World War, I was the first of my immediate family ever to "go past high school," as people where I come from used to say (my older brother's educational trajectory was detoured by the *Second* World War), and on the whole I regard my apprenticeship in academe as both benevolent and beneficial indeed, although even at the time I half-appreciated that literature had managed nicely for several millennia without the benefit of creative-writing programs and would doubtless continue to struggle along somehow if they should all disappear tomorrow. ("At the time" here means the late 1940s, when the then-new program at Johns Hopkins, which recently turned 50, was only the second degree-granting writing program in our republic—second after Iowa's. At last count the number exceeded 400, I believe, but

The Hopwood Lecture, 1998

I stand by my proposition.) I shall circle back, perhaps, to a hedged defense of this almost uniquely American, post-World War II phenomenon, the college creative-writing program, and of the concomitant phenomenon of poets and fictionists as professors. I bring the matter up now in order to launch the following reminiscence by way of reply to Question #1: "Why bother, etc.?" It is an anecdote that I've told elsewhere; kindly indulge its twice-telling,

My then-closest graduate-school-fellow-apprentice-writer-friend and I, as we were about to be duly certified by our university as Masters of Arts despite our still-considerable distance from anything resembling mastery, considered together what we might do to pay the rent until the golden shower of literary fame and fortune descended upon us. Having had some school-vacation experience of such alternatives as factory-, sales-, and clerical work as well as manual labor, we agreed by passionate default that *college teaching* looked to be the least abusive of our available options and potentially the richest in free time for writing. It had not escaped our notice that doctors, lawyers, administrators, and businessfolk, for example, tend to get busier as their careers advance, whereas the work-loads of university professors in the humanities appeared to us to get progressively lighter and more flexible as they ascend the academic ranks. Never mind whether this perception was correct; my buddy and I were persuaded enough thereby to decide to become writer/teachers: Writers in the University. Inasmuch as we ourselves had been blessed with splendid professors of a great many disciplines and were the opposite of cynical about the teaching half of our prospective double careers, our next consideration was how we might spend our classroom time most fruitfully for our students-to-be and ourselves. My friend—who had a stronger intellectual string to his bow than I and a more solid background in literature, history, and philosophy—decided that he would devote *his* academic life to the answering of rhetorical questions. Should one of his future students happen to ask blithely, for example, "Who's to say, finally, what's real and what isn't?" Ben vowed that he would tap himself on the chest and lead that student rigorously through the history of metaphysics, from the pre-Socratics up to the current semester.

And I? Well, the Answering of All Rhetorical Questions is no easy act to follow—Wouldn't you agree?—but it occurred to me to vow in my turn that I would spend *my* academic life saying over and over again All the Things That Go Without Saying; that (if I may paraphrase myself) I would stare first principles and basic distinctions out of countenance; face them down, for my students' benefit and my own, until they blink and confess new information. What is literature? What is fiction? What is a *story?*

And so for the next many years I did, and indeed continue still to do, although the dialogue is more often with myself these emeritus days than with students. And I hope to return to at least the last of those examples (What is a story?) later in this talk. So that's two things now to be perhaps returned to, the first being . . . I forget what, but trust that *it* will return to *me.* Meanwhile, having answered or at least responded to my opening question—"Why bother to attempt serious replies to banal questions?"—I now proceed to a few of those questions themselves.

That gifted graduate-school pal, alas, died young leaving many rhetorical questions still unanswered. In faithful pursuit of our jointly-declared program, however, I've been writing more fiction as well as professing it ever since, and publishing it for 40-plus years or 5000-plus pages, whichever is longer, and giving public readings from it (most often on college campuses) for at least 35 of those 40 years at the rate of about one reading per month in the academic season, for the pleasure of trying out my sentences on a live audience instead of a merely living one (I should perhaps confess that it was as a more or less failed jazz musician that I came to fiction-writing). More often than not, these monthly gigs include responding to questions from the audience afterward—something that for better or worse a writer doesn't normally get to do with his or her readers.

As you might imagine, over the semesters at least a few of those questions come to be fairly expectable and not inherently exciting—*Do you write your books with a pen or a pencil or what? Have any of your novels been made into movies? What effect, if any, has your university teaching had on your writing?* Whether or not such routine questions—and my earnest responses thereto—are interesting, it *has* interested me to see both the questions and the replies evolve somewhat over the decades. Taking them in order (I mean in order to get them out of our way):

1. The old question *Do you write with a pen or a pencil or a typewriter or what?* changed about a dozen years ago to *typewriter or word processor?* and nowadays it seems to have become *desktop or laptop?*—as if that exhausts the imaginable options any more than does the classic "Your place or mine?" I have never understood the great pen-or-pencil

question's point, so to speak, in either its low-tech or its higher-tech versions, but I'm impressed by its frequency. Is the asker an aspiring writer, I wonder, who imagines that a change of instruments might induce the muse to sing? Can she or he be thinking, "Since that guy uses Microsoft Word 5.0 on an old Macintosh LCIII and his stuff gets published and even remains by and large in print, perhaps if [etc.]. . ." It's a magic syllogism. Even if the question's motive is less complimentary, its logic is no less fallacious: "Ah, so: He writes with a Mont Blanc Meisterstück fountain pen. That explains the Germanic interminability of certain of his novels," etc.

No, no, no, dear interrogator: You must seek elsewhere the explanation of their Germanic *und so weiter.* What earthly difference can it make to the muses whether one composes one's sentences with a Cray mainframe supercomputer or with the big toe of one's left foot (like the cerebrally palsied Irish writer Shane Connaught) or with one's nose or with some other appendage of one's anatomy or for that matter of someone else's anatomy? It goes without saying—Does it not?—that those sentences are what they are, for better or worse, whatever the instrument of their setting down.

I do remember, however, once hearing the critic Hugh Kenner speak in an interesting way of how literature changed after the nineteenth century when it came to be composed on typewriters instead of penned, its alphabetical atoms no longer cursively linked within their verbal molecules (these metaphors are mine, not Professor Kenner's) but ineluctably and forever side-by-siding like wary subway passengers, and leached of individual calligraphy as well. When I objected that a few antediluvians, such as my erstwhile Baltimore neighbor Anne Tyler and myself, still prefer the muscular cursive of longhand penmanship for first-drafting our prose, Kenner replied, "All the same, you grew up breathing the air of literature composed on the typewriter." Well, he had me there, sort of—except that the air that most oxygenated my particular apprenticeship was a fairly equal mix of high Modernism (presumably typewritten) and of quill-scrawled antiquity, with a healthy component of the oral tale-telling tradition as well. It is a mixture that I heartily recommend to apprentice writers: one foot in the high-tech topical here and now, one foot in narrative antiquity, and a third foot, if you can spare it, in the heroic middle distance.

My favorite response to the classic pen/pencil/Powerbook question, you'll be excited to hear, comes in fact from those older storytelling traditions. The enormous Sanskrit tale-cycle *Kathā Sarit Sāgara,* or Ocean of Streams of Story, was set down in the tenth or eleventh century—with a quill pen, presumably—by the Kashmirian court poet Somadeva. Its ten large folio volumes pretend to be a radical *abridgment* of the surviving *one-seventh* of what has to have been in its original version the longest story ever told or written: the *Brīhat Kathā,* or Great Tale, first told by the god Shiva to his consort Parvati as a thank-you gift for a particularly divine session of lovemaking. By my calculations (based on what's conjectured about the Homeric oral tradition), it must have taken Shiva two and a half years to spin the thing out, while Parvati sat listening patiently on his lap—the primordial laptop, I suppose. No problem in their case, since the tale, the teller, and the told were all immortal. But when Shiva's Great Tale was first written down by the scribe Gunadhya (so our later writer Somadeva declares), its passage from the oral to the written medium required seven full years—which is just as well, inasmuch as the medium of transcription was the scribe's own blood.

So it is, more or less, my friends, with all of us: a good case for writing short stories and lyric poems, perhaps, unless your blood-replacement capacity is that of an Anne Rice male lead. Just as Senator Daniel Patrick Moynihan suggested a few years ago that the efficient cause of American violence isn't guns but ammunition, so maybe the pen/pencil/Powerbook question ought to be *Skrip, Quink, ribbon, bubble-jet, or laser? Blood-group O, A, or B?* There is much more, by the way, to that exemplary *Kathāpitha,* or Story of the Story, as Volume One of Somadeva's ten-volume abridgment of the surviving one-seventh of The Ocean of Story is called. But I don't want to spoil the pleasure of your reading the whole thing for yourself.

Once upon a time a quarter-century ago, as I was driving the poet John Ashbery to his scheduled reading-plus-Q & A at Johns Hopkins, he wondered aloud to me what sort of questions he was likely to be asked. "The usual, no doubt," I assured him: *"Do you write with a pen or a pencil?,* stuff like that." "Oh, I hope they ask *that* one," Ashbery said; "*I like* that one!"

Truth to tell, so do I. To get right down to it, breath-bated auditors, I write my fiction with an immortal British Parker 51 fountain pen bought three dozen years ago in honor of the great Charles Dickens in what is alleged to be Mister Pumblechook's premises in Rochester, England; that instrument is charged with Scheaffer's Skrip and deployed in the looseleaf binder—battered but still-functioning, like its owner—that

I bought during freshman orientation week at Johns Hopkins in September 1947. From there, at morning's end, the day's "muscular cursive" is Macintoshed for extensive editing and revision. And I compose my nonfiction, this lecture included, mainly on Fridays, with a MontBlanc Meisterstück 146 fountain pen bequeathed me by a beloved Spanish friend and critic upon his untimely death from stomach cancer, he having chosen for his epitaph this line from a story of mine about a skeptical spermatozoon: "It is we spent old swimmers, disabused of every illusion, who are most vulnerable to dreams." And I deploy that Meisterstück in an altogether different, history-free looseleaf binder before Macintoshing et cetera. Lately, however, I seem to've taken to nonficting directly on the word-processor, without that muscular-cursive foreplay. Make of that datum what you will.

2. Q: *Have any of your novels been made into movies?*

A: I always used to answer *No* to that question, even when some film buff claimed to have seen *The End of the Road* back in the early 1970s with Stacey Keach playing Jacob Homer, Harris Yulin as Joe Morgan, Dorothy Tristan as Rennie Morgan, and James Earl Jones as the capital-D Doctor. Despite my name in the credits and my modest payment for the film rights, I deny that that wretched flick has anything to do with my rigorous little novel of the same title and dramatis personae. (The movie critic John Simon declared at the time, correctly, that the principal difference between the novel and film versions of the story is that whereas my novel concludes with a harrowing abortion, the film is a harrowing abortion from start to finish.) But what was the question *for?,* I used to wonder, as I did with the pen-or-pencil one. I couldn't help translating it to mean, "Reading's a drag, man, but I dig movies, so I'll maybe catch you out at the nabes and see if you're on my wavelength."

As you can tell from that vintage slang, the question as given is dated. Its current version would be, "Are any of your novels available as videos?" The answer is still No, and I can't recommend the audiocassette versions, either. The updated question, I fear, has to be translated, "Hauling out to the Cineplex has gotten to be almost as much of a bummer as reading books, but I do like to slug the old VCR if there's nothing on Cable."

What can a mere novelist say? Echoing Robert Frost's famous

definition of poetry as "that which gets lost in translation," my comrade-in-arms William Gass defines *story* as "that which is extracted from a novel to make a movie." I agree, I guess, although for me the element of story remains first among equals in the ingredients of fiction. But in a good novel (it goes without saying) the story is truly inseparable from the language it's told in and the voice that tells it. Movies are, literally, another story altogether, and videocassettes another story yet. As it happens, the best I can say even for a good movie-adaptation of a good novel—such as Anthony Minghella's film of Michael Ondaatje's *The English Patient*—is what Thomas Mann said about reading Shakespeare in German translation: "It's like taking a hundred thousand dollars from a millionaire," Mann declared: "He remains a very rich man."

It now appears evident that what movies and network television did to live theater earlier in this century (not to mention what they did to the audience for printed fiction), the VCR and cable TV are doing to the movie houses and to some extent to the film industry. That's just a fact of technological life. Of more interest to me is a different analogy: If movies and television have affected the art of prose fiction in the twentieth century in something like the way that still photography affected the art of painting in the latter nineteenth, then we can reasonably expect that the development of interactive television and high-tech "virtualism" in the century to come will have a comparable effect on movies and videos as we know them today. We are told by another of my American comrades-in-arms, Robert Coover, that electronic fiction and computer hypertext generally will have a comparable revolutionary impact on what remains of printed-book culture, with its obsolescent notions of author, reader, text, publisher, copyright, and the like. I confess that I won't at all regret missing that particular technological revolution, which along with electronic virtuality offers to do to the audience for "p-fiction" what the rise of the novel since the seventeenth century did to the audience for poetry. It gives me some comfort to note, however, that while in my lifetime I've had to replace my 78 rpm records with 45s and then with 33.3 LPs, and then those with audiocassettes and then those with compact disks, each time discarding and expensively rebuilding my recorded-music library, the oldest volumes in my *book* library remain by and large as conveniently accessible as they were on their publication-day, perhaps centuries ago. If fewer and fewer people read printed fiction in the century to come, that won't be because the marvelously low-tech, high-protein medium of the book is outmoded, but because the pleasures of reading will have been displaced by glitzy and evanescent high-tech distractions for which civilization will be on balance the poorer. If thus it must go, then I shall with some small relief go first.

That curmudgeonly sentiment brings me to the last of these evolving but nevertheless routine questions, after which we'll move on to a couple of less routine ones and then have done.

3. Q: *What effect does your university teaching have on your novels?*

A: My reply to this gee-whizzer used to be, "it delays their completion." In this case, however, although the question remains the same, the respondent's altered circumstances require a different answer. As afore-established, I was indeed for four decades a full-time teacher as well as a full-time writer, and for the first two of those four decades I was a full-time parent as well—when you're young, you can full-time it on several fronts at once. Then my children grew up and (just as my late friend and I had foretold) my academic workload eased off, so that for several years I taught only one semester out of two, and for a few years after that only one graduate-level seminar every second semester. More lately, for the first time since kindergarten I've been out of the classroom altogether. To my total unsurprise, in these progressively time-richer circumstances my literary output has remained almost exactly what it was forty years ago, when I was teaching four sections of freshman composition, six days a week, and helping to raise three small children, and moonlighting in a dance band on weekends for extra cash. Back then I stole time to write, and my larceny was sufficiently grand that I was able to go straight later on. Now that I have all the writing-time I want—in a day, in a week, in a year, if never in a lifetime—I find that although I enjoy generating sentences and stories as much as ever, I don't spend any more time at it than I did when I wished that I had a lot more time to spend. One's musely metabolism, evidently, is what it is almost regardless of circumstances, and so I infer that what used to delay the completion of my novels was not university teaching after all; it was (and it remains) living that part of life that doesn't consist of writing fiction—the part of life without which, in my case anyhow, there wouldn't be any fiction to write, even though that fiction seldom has to do directly with its author's biographical experience.

Does that, too, go without saying, I wonder? In any case, there it is: said.

So much for those profoundly routine questions, which I seem to find routinely profound. Of the non-routine sort I shall instance just one, and then ask myself one myself, and then we're done. Now and then, in the post-reading or post-lectorial Q & A, someone will come up with something at least as perceptive, and on occasion as unsettling, as anything that my most learned and attentive critics have laid on me. It was an anonymous member of some audience a quarter-century ago who in the Q & A observed that my books thus far (of which there were back then only six) tended to come in *pairs,* the second member of each pair a sort of complement or corrective to the first; inasmuch as the questioner understood me to be one half of a pair of opposite-sex twins, she wondered how programmatic on my part might be this metaphor of more-or-less-paired books, and what I took to be its significance.

Well, I was floored; had never until that moment noticed what now seemed evident, even conspicuous—the more so since the theme of twinship itself comes up in a couple of those books. Moreover, although I've never regarded my twin sister and me as complements other than anatomically, and certainly not as reciprocal correctives, I was so intrigued, even charmed by the unintended metaphor that I resolved perversely to defy it. And so I did in Book #7 (a monster novel called *LETTERS),* to which the slender novel that followed it had only the most tenuous connection; and Book #9, a collection of essays, was surely no twin to either of those—so there. But then Book #10, I noticed after writing it, can fairly be regarded as dizygotic not to Book #9 but to Book #8, and Books 11 and 12 to each other, and Book 13 (a second essay-collection) to the aforementioned Book 9, and Book 14 (a story-series) as trizygotic to Book 5 on the one hand and to Book 15 (another story-series, currently in progress) on the other, and so it would appear that only that gargantuan *Mittelpunkt,* Book #7, remains (so far) untwinned—although, come to think of it, it contains within its intrications sequels to all six of its predecessors. . . . Make of all this, too, what you will; I myself have come to shrug my shoulders—first the left, and then, complementarily, the right. . .

Let us return to the country of Things That Go Without Saying. One Q that I've never had a chance to A in these public circumstances is the perhaps most basic and apparently elementary of all—which is why I used frequently to put it to my coachees (especially the most advanced apprentice writers among them), and why I put it still to myself, most often in the well-filling interval between books: What is fiction? What's a *story?*

Okay, so that's two questions, really, and for the *long* replies thereto I refer anyone who's interested to an essay of mine called "It Goes Without Saying," in the collection *Further Fridays*—one of those dizygotic twin volumes afore-referred-to. The *short* answer to the question "What's a story?" was provided me by some member of yet another audience past, who after the show pressed upon me a treatise on something called Systems Philosophy and urged me to read it on the flight home. As I had no idea what Systems Philosophy might be, I did indeed leaf through that gift-book up there in the stratosphere, and although I landed not much wiser as to its subject, it did provide me with some wonderful jargon, out of which I constructed the following rigorous definition of the term *story:* A story (it goes without saying) consists of *the incremental perturbation of an unstable homeostatic system and its catastrophic restoration to a complexified equilibrium.*

I confess to being in love with that definition—which in fact quite accurately describes classic Aristotelian dramaturgy. The "unstable homeostatic system" is what I've called elsewhere the Ground Situation of any story: a dramaturgically voltaged state of affairs pre-existing the story's present action, like the ongoing feud between the Capulets and the Montagues. Its "incremental perturbation" is the "rising action" or complications of the conflict following upon the introduction of a Dramatic Vehicle into the Ground Situation (Romeo Montague and Juliet Capulet fall into star-crossed love, a turn of events that precipitates Bandello's tale and Shakespeare's play out of the Ground Situation; the couple's incrementally more desperate attempts to consummate that love comprise the story's action). The "catastrophic restoration" is the climax or Aristotelian peripeteia, catastrophic in its relative swiftness and magnitude even in the quietest of stories. And the "complexified equilibrium" thereby restored is the classic denouement, dramaturgically consequential vis-à-vis the original Ground Situation or else no story has been told or sung or written down or played out (the lovers' death, e.g., puts the interfamily squabble at least temporarily on Hold).

All that sort of thing really does go without saying for most storytellers, who work at least as much by the hunch and feel of experienced talent as by articulated theory, and who are likely to find it easier to make up a story than to explain the difference between stories and non-stories or not-quite stories. If such high-tech theorizing makes no more sense to you than, say, much of life does, then I offer you another pet maxim from my inventory, to wit: *Of of what one can't make sense, one may make art.* May I repeat those eleven quasi stammering monosyllables? *Of of what one can't make sense, one may make art.*

O self-demonstrating bliss.

But why *does* one make art? Specifically, what accounts for the odd circumstance that people in every time and place appear to enjoy, whether as individuals or as cultures, making up nonfactual yarns, for example, and telling or writing or acting them out and hearing or reading or spectating them? Why is it that we Homo sapienses pleasure in the incremental perturbation of imaginary unstable homeostatic systems and their catastrophic restoration to complexified equilibria? In the vicarious turning of screws on cooked-up predicaments until those quantitative increments effect a comparatively sudden and significant qualitative change?

Damned if I know. In the Friday-piece mentioned above ("It Goes Without Saying") I itemized some two dozen of fiction's feasible functions, from reality-testing and -mapping to reality-avoidance, from aphrodisia through anaphrodisia to mere linguistical futzing around. Behind all of those catalogued functions, I believe (as well as any of the many that I no doubt missed), lies a neuroscientific argument that strikes me as both plausible and pleasing, and with which I'll close my spiel. The self-styled "neurophilosopher" Daniel C. Dennett, of Tufts University, maintains that human consciousness itself has an essentially narrative aspect, grounded in the biological evolution of the brain. I won't attempt here to summarize Dennett's thesis, but I am immediately persuaded of its validity—at least as an explanatory fiction. To me it seems a short and plausible step, though a consequential and doubtless an intricate one, from the "if" propositions characteristic of computer and neural programming—*If x, then y,* etc., which in animal behavior might be called the Four F-propositions: whether Stimulus or Situation X prompts us to Flee, Fight, Feed, or, you know, Mate—it's a short and plausible step, I was saying, from these to the *what ifs* and *as ifs* of fictional narrative. I second the motion that the "neural Darwinism" by which consciousness may evolve—evolve not only to recognize and act upon stimuli but to reflect upon, disport with, and be moved to aesthetic pleasure by certain of them—has an inherently narrative aspect. Professor Dennett goes even farther, conceiving of consciousness as essentially a "multi-draft scenario spinner," or "Joycean machine"; of the self itself as an *as if,* a "posited Center of Narrative Gravity"—in short, as an intricate onspinning fiction. "We *are* the stories we tell ourselves and others about who we are," he concludes (in his treatise *Consciousness Explained*): stories that we edit continually, and that continually edit us.

Amen to that, say I. Whether or not one goes the whole way with Dennett's neurophilosophy (and some very prominent neuroscientists do not), he has I think established at very least that when we make up stories or take pleasure in made-up stories, we are literally doing what comes naturally.

Now, then, I ask you: Did the pondering of questions like these ever make anybody a better writer? Wouldn't any fictionist be just as well off following the example of Norman Mailer, say, who in his 1984 Hopwood Lecture declared his tendency "to mumble about technical matters like an old mechanic"? "'Let's put the thingamajig before the whoosits here'," said Mailer, "is how I usually state the deepest literary problems to myself." Same here, more often than not, when I am in actual intimate congress with the muse. It's in the recovery-time between such sessions that I incline to put such questions more formally to myself and to entertain them from others. And I happen to believe that when we do *that,* too, we're doing what comes naturally—perhaps more naturally to some people than to others.

But I suppose that that goes without saying.

Any further questions?